O9-BUC-103

Please remember that this is a library book,
and that it belongs only temporarily to each
person who uses it. Be considerate. Do
not write in this, or any, library book.

WITHDRAWN

CHILDREN OF POVERTY

STUDIES ON THE EFFECTS
OF SINGLE PARENTHOOD,
THE FEMINIZATION OF POVERTY,
AND HOMELESSNESS

edited by

STUART BRUCHEY
UNIVERSITY OF MAINE

A GARLAND SERIES

167609
VC Grad
GP-MA

RUNAWAY ADOLESCENTS

A FAMILY SYSTEMS PERSPECTIVE

WITHDRAWN

BRENDA K. MELSON

GARLAND PUBLISHING, INC.
NEW YORK & LONDON / 1995

Copyright © 1995 Brenda K. Melson
All rights reserved

Library of Congress Cataloging-in-Publication Data

Melson, Brenda K., 1941–
    Runaway adolescents : a family systems perspective / Brenda
K. Melson.
        p.   cm. — (Children of poverty)
    Includes bibliographical references (p. 262) and index.
    ISBN 0-8153-2334-4 (alk. paper)
    1. Runaway teenagers—United States. 2. Family psycho-
therapy. I. Title. II. Series.
HV1431.M38 1995   95-25280
362.7'4—dc20

Printed on acid-free, 250-year-life paper
Manufactured in the United States of America

To my husband,

my parents,

my children,

and

my granddaughter,

who've made home a place I always love to be

Please remember that this is a library book,
and that it belongs only temporarily to each
person who uses it. Be considerate. Do
not write in this, or any, library book.

CONTENTS

PREFACE

Work for this book began in the middle 1980s while I served as part-time counselor at a private agency in the city of St. Louis and pursued doctoral study at St. Louis University. Children and adolescents, many of whom were runaways, and their parents were among those referred to the counseling agency by the Status Offender Unit of the St. Louis Police Department. My work with runaways and their parents, in conjunction with my doctoral study in the Department of Education with a concentration in Marriage and Family Development and Therapy, provided opportunities to apply family systems theory to clinical work with runaways in their family context. This effort led to my doctoral dissertation and later to additional research and publication of this book.

Current estimates of adolescent runaways range between one and two million per year, and predictions are that the phenomenon will remain a major concern in this country for years to come. Much contradictory and confusing evidence regarding adolescent runaway behavior appears to be hindering the formation of meaningful social policy as well as effective prevention, treatment, and research strategies. Today's runaways are quite different from those runaways who were among American's earliest immigrants and from runaways who were common during periods of war and social upheaval throughout American history. This study proposes family systems theory as a comprehensive theoretical framework which can be applied meaningfully to understanding the complex adolescent runaway phenomenon. This framework should prove useful to practitioners and service providers in their understanding and treatment of runaways, to educators and counselors in their teaching and guidance of adolescents, and to researchers in their further study of the adolescent runaway phenomenon.

The design of this study is historical, theoretical, and case study. From the historical perspective, the runaway literature is examined and major themes summarized. From the theoretical perspective, systems theory in general and key concepts of the theory as it applies to families are outlined. Case examples are presented to demonstrate the applicability of family systems theory to the adolescent runaway phenomenon. Suggestions for further study are presented.

ACKNOWLEDGMENTS

I would never have begun this project, much less have completed it, without the unwavering support of my family. My heartfelt appreciation goes to my husband, Dr. G. Leland Melson, for his confidence in me as well as his patience, assistance, and encouragement throughout my years of study and now to his happy memory. I am grateful to my son John and his wife Allison, my son David and his wife Angela, and my daughter Sarah for their understanding and encouragement for as long as they can remember. I offer thanks to my parents, Martha and Wooodrow Hardin, for giving me a lifetime of nurturance and affirmation. I extend my deepest gratitude to all for their sharing this experience, for their pride in my endeavors, and, most of all, for their love. To other family members, colleagues, and dear friends near and far who are part of my extended family system I offer my appreciation for their loving care, confidence, and support.

For development of my doctoral dissertation and production of this book itself I am deeply grateful:

–to Dr. John K. DiTiberio, advisor and chairperson of my dissertation committee, for his guidance, assistance, and support;

–to Dr. Raymond A. Carroll and Dr. J. Douglas Petinelli, dissertation committee members, for their suggestions and encouragement;

–to Dr. Raphael J. Becvar and Dr. Dorothy Stroh Becvar for their inspiration as teachers throughout my doctoral study, for their confidence in me, and for their friendship;

–to Elspeth Hart and Robert McKenzie, editors at Garland, for their guidance and suggestions; and

–to my son David for offering his technical expertise, assistance, and availability day and night to keep me on the right track.

Runaway Adolescents

I

Introduction

BACKGROUND

In 1975, Walker[1] stated:

It is difficult to summarize the multidisciplinary literature on runaway youth into a sound theoretical framework from which a meaningful social policy can be formulated. This difficulty is attributable mainly to the lack of a broad conceptual framework which is comprehensive enough to incorporate the disparate views on runaways cited in the literature. Without such a framework . . . it is impossible to integrate and/or compare meaningfully all the findings of the various studies (p. 6).

By 1989, Burke and Burkhead also claimed that "while youths running away from home have been the focus of a good deal of research, there remains considerable confusion regarding runaway behavior. . . . The findings from the literature are difficult to integrate into a coherent theoretical development of runaway behavior".[2]

Walker[3] concluded that the two main characteristics of the literature she reviewed which aggravate the problem are:

. . . the lack of a consistent definition(s) of runaways across studies, and the lack of a methodological sophistication in many studies. Part of the reason for these problems is the nature of the runaway phenomenon itself. "Running away" is a complex psychological and sociological problem which is difficult to define, explain, and therefore study. A third reason for the problem is the differences and diversity of the various disciplines' vocabularies, theories, and biases. It is always hard to integrate many disciplines' orientations to a problem or phenomenon into a framework that will be understandable and useful as a whole, as well as still accountable to all the individual disciplines. (p. 6)

In her suggestions for future research Walker encouraged "interdisciplinary teams to study runaway youth in order to foster maximum integration of the various disparate views on treating and understanding runaway youth" (p. 33). Because of inconclusive evidence for explaining runaway behavior within one theoretical context, Walker encouraged researchers to "adopt a relatively open-minded   position which   recognizes the importance of both internal and external factors in explaining runaway behavior" (p. 33).

Gulotta[4] believed that there existed a need to reexamine the whole issue of runaways. He said that:

. . . suggesting that these youngsters demonstrate characteristics indicative of severe pathology is erroneous. . . A narrowly defined understanding of the child leaving home, one which places responsibility for the act on the child alone, indicates the need for a much wider study of this complex phenomenon (p. 114).

The   lack of separating one-time runaways from repeat runaways, the lack of sophisticated methodology in many studies, and contradictory findings of the present literature are several factors which have hindered the development of a coherent theory, according to Burke and Burkhead.[5] Like Walker and Gulotta, they believed that such problems are due in part to the runaway phenomenon's being a complex problem that has been difficult to define or explain.

Many other researchers have come to similar conclusions. Although increased attention, concern, and research have been devoted to runaways, the understanding of running away remains limited and inconclusive, resulting in a continuing debate regarding the etiology of this behavior.[6]

A challenging problem that continues to escalate in number each year and plague the social conscience of society at large is runaway children . . . . Clearly, the problem is complex and research efforts to demonstrate cause-and-effect have not shown definitive results. Indeed, it is becoming obvious that the runaway phenomenon may not lend itself to the prescriptiveness of cause-and-effect explanations because there are multisystems involved in the lives of children who leave home and of the parents.[7]

THE PROBLEM

A preliminary search of the literature reveals that the formation of a meaningful social policy as well as the development of appropriate and effective prevention, treatment and research strategies toward adolescent runaways appears to be hindered by the lack of a broad theoretical framework which would encompass the complex phenomenon of runaway behavior. Being neither a creation of the turbulent 1960s nor a minor passing fad, the concept of the adolescent period in our society, specifically runaway adolescents, is now and will continue to be a major concern for years to come. Often our society labels runaway children as either psychopathological or delinquent (or perhaps both). Yet a review of the history of running away in America provides much contradictory evidence.[8]

A need to narrow the gap of knowledge concerning this phenomenon and the need for a comprehensive theoretical framework which can be meaningfully applied to its understanding appear evident. A theory which addresses the difficulties of cause-and-effect explanations and also the importance of the multisystems involved in the lives of adolescent runaways is family systems theory. This theory addresses individual phenomenon from a contextual framework, and shows promise for being extremely useful in understanding the complex phenomenon of adolescents running away from home and, further, in developing appropriate prevention, treatment, and research strategies.

NEED FOR THE STUDY

Walker's comprehensive review of the literature on runaways through 1974 and Burke and Burkhead's more limited review concluded that neither a broad conceptual framework nor a coherent theory of runaway behavior existed. A further review of the literature to the present time has not shown much more in the way of the development of such a theoretical framework. These findings and the potential usefulness of a unifying theory point to the need for the present study which will attempt to partially fill the gap in the understanding of the runaway phenomenon.

Adopting a systems approach, other writers and researchers have focused on families and family therapy, including concerns about adolescent runaways. Stierlin, Fishman, and Mirkin, Raskin and Antognini, for example, focus on practical methodologies for family therapy. Stierlin focuses on the theme of the separation process of adolescents and their parents. He develops his interactional concepts of centripetal and centrifugal forces which are evidenced in the family and refers to the problems of runaways in the context of the adolescent separation process. Crespi and Sabatelli view running away as a conflict-induced effort by the youth to evolve a differentiated self when embedded within an individuation-inhibiting family system. Fishman focuses on clinical cases of a number of troubled adolescents of which the runaway is one. He presents case studies in the areas of delinquency, the violent family, incest, suicide, and disability as well as the runaway. Stierlin, Fishman, and Mirkin, Raskin and Antognini propose family therapy as a basic approach. Their major emphasis is more pragmatic and practical than theoretical, and, for Stierlin and Fishman, the runaway phenomenon was not the primary focus. Mirkin, Raskin and Antognini focused on families of adolescent female runaways.[9]

To this point, however, no one has conducted a comprehensive review of the literature on runaways from the 1970s to the present in order to discover themes and patterns which could be understood within a theoretical perspective comprehensive enough to incorporate the disparate views which exist.

PURPOSE OF THE STUDY

The purpose of this study is to conduct a comprehensive review of the literature on runaways which will partially fill the gap in knowledge of them and to offer family systems theory as a broad theoretical perspective with which to better understand the runaway phenomenon. Such a perspective should prove useful to practitioners and service providers in their understanding and treatment of runaways, to educators and counselors in their teaching and guidance of adolescents, and to researchers in their further study of the runaway phenomenon. The theoretical perspective to be examined which appears to hold most promise for understanding runaways is that of family systems theory.

HYPOTHESIS AND METHOD

It is the conceptual hypothesis of this study that family systems theory is a useful, comprehensive theoretical framework for the understanding of the complex phenomenon of runaway behavior. The purpose of this study will be to:

1) conduct a comprehensive review of the literature on runaways to date giving particular attention to summarizing major aspects of the phenomenon which appear across the studies;

2) define and describe some key concepts of family systems theory which may be applicable to the study of the runaway phenomenon;

3) discuss and link the key principles of one theoretical model, family systems theory, to the phenomenon of runaway behavior;

4) discuss case illustrations from the literature which demonstrate the usefulness of the family systems model to the understanding and treatment of runaways; and

5) discuss implications for research, prevention, and treatment which are consistent with the framework of family systems theory.

DESIGN

The design of this project is historical, theoretical, and case study. In the historical aspect, the literature on the runaway phenomenon will be examined and major themes summarized. From the theoretical perspective, systems theory in general and key concepts of the theory as it applies to families will be outlined. Case illustrations will be presented to demonstrate in concrete terms the applicability of family systems theory to adolescent runaways and, in that manner, determine the validity of the hypothesis.

ORGANIZATION

A comprehensive review of the literature on runaways will follow this introductory chapter in Chapter Two. Several major aspects of the runaway phenomenon which emerged from the literature will be discussed in depth:

History

Definition

Incidence/Occurrence/Description

Reasons/Predisposing Factors

Typologies/Classification Systems

Recommendations for Prevention and Treatment

Suggestions for Future Research and Evaluation.

Chapter Three will address some key concepts of systems theory, all of which apply to families and to the various models of systemic family therapy. Several models of systemic family therapy will be described briefly in order to demonstrate the variety of approaches which are found within the framework of systems theory. Discussion of the key family systems theory concepts will be linked to the phenomenon of runaway behavior.

Case illustrations will be examined in Chapter Four as a means of determining the validity of the hypothesis.

The final chapter will summarize the results of this study and cite its limitations. Suggestions for further research, prevention, and treatment will be presented.

NOTES

[1] D. Walker, *Runaway Youth: Annotated Bibliography and Literature Overview* (Washington, D.C.: Office of Social Services and Human Development, Department of Health and Human Services, 1975).

[2] W. Burke and E. Burkhead, "Runaway Children in America: A Review of the Literature," *Education and Treatment of Children* 12 (February 1989), p. 73.

[3] See note 1 above.

[4] T. Gulotta, "Leaving Home: Family Relationships of the Runaway Child," *Social Casework: The Journal of Contemporary Social Work* (February 1979): 111-114.

[5] See note 2 above.

[6] D. Adams and G. Munro, "Portrait of the North American Runaway: A Critical Review," *Journal of Youth and Adolescence* 8 (Fall 1979): 359-373; T. Brennan, D. Huizinga and D. Elliott, *The Social Psychology of Runaways* (Lexington, MA: D.C. Heath and Co., 1978); T. Brennan, "Mapping the Diversity Among Runaways: A Descriptive Multivatiate Analysis of Selected Social Psychological Background Conditions," *Journal of Family Issues* 1 ((June 1980): 189-209; K. Libertoff, "The Runaway Child in America: A Social History," *Journal of Family Issues* 1 (June 1980): 151-164.

[7] E. Spillane-Grieco, "Characteristics of a Helpful Relationship: A Study of Empathic Understanding and Positive Regard Between Runaways and Their Parents," *Adolescence* XIX (1984): 63-75.

[8] See note 2 above; R. Shellow, J. Schamp, E. Liebow and E. Unger, "Suburban Runaways of the 1960's," *Monograph of the Society for Research in Child Development* 32 (1967):1-50; See note 1 above.

[9] H. Stierlin, "A Family Perspective on Adolescent Runaways," *Archives of General Psychiatry* 29 (July 1973): 56-62; H. Stierlin, *Separating Parents and Adolescents* (New York: Jason Aronson, Inc., 1981); H. Fishman, *Treating Troubled Adolescents*

(New York: Basic Books, 1988); M. Mirkin, P. Raskin and F. Antognini, "Parenting, Protecting, Preserving: Mission of the Adolescent Female Runaway," *Family Process* 23 (March 1984): 63-74; D. Crespi and R. Sabatelli, "Adolescent Runaways and Family Strife: A Conflict-Induced Differentiation Framework," *Adolescence* 28 (Winter 1993): 867-878.

II

Literature Review

INTRODUCTION

Deborah Klein Walker's 1975 technical analysis paper entitled "Runaway Youth: An Annotated Bibliography and Literature Overview"[1] was prepared for the Department of Health, Education, and Welfare, now the Department of Health and Human Services. The major questions Walker addressed were:

1) Who are the runaways? How is "runaway" best defined?

2) What is the incidence (i.e., rate of occurrence) of running away?

3) What are the predisposing factors which lead to youths running away?

4) What services are available to runaway youth and their families? Of these, which are effective?

5) What are the various attitudes towards runningaway in American society? Within the context of the differing approaches to the phenomenon, what are the most desirable policies (in term of services provided, legal regulations, etc.) (p.1).

Walker's paper was prepared following the 1974 appropriation of funds by Congress and prior to the formulation of policies towards runaways. She gathered information from 156 sources from both the professional and popular literature on runaway youth. These sources included books, professional journals, government documents, popular magazines, and newspaper articles.

In 1985 the National Network of Runaway and Youth Services, Inc. published a report entitled "To Whom Do They Belong?" subtitled "A Profile of America's Runaway and Homeless Youth and the Programs That Help Them." Data for this report were compiled from information provided by 210 runaway and homeless youth services programs which responded to an eight page survey. The purpose of the report was to analyze the survey's findings, draw some "first-level conclusions," and raise some issues for consideration by service providers, policy makers, and concerned citizens.[2]

Dozens of articles and research studies on runaways have appeared in the literature up to the present time. The findings will be reviewed here under the following categories:

History
Definition
Incidence/Occurrence/Description
Reasons/Predisposing Factors
Typologies/Classification Systems
Recommendations for Prevention and Treatment
Suggestions for Future Research and Evaluation

HISTORY

American society has always had young people who run away from home. Runaway children were among the earliest immigrants to America during the seventeenth and eighteenth centuries. They were "familiar fixtures" in the settlement and development of the original 13 colonies and, throughout American history, periods of war and social upheaval have always spurred runaway activity.[3]

Some of the most well-known popularized examples of runaway youth are Huckleberry Finn and Tom Sawyer in frontier Missouri, the wandering groups of transient boys of the depression years, and the hippies or "flower children" of the late 1960s.[4] Their paths may not have been easy, but eventually most youth returned to their families and assumed more appropriate adult behavior.

Justice and Duncan[5] pointed out that these fantasies of the past pale in comparison to the realities of the present. They quoted from a report by former Senator Birch Bayh:

> Unlike Mark Twain's era, running away today is a phenomenon of our cities. Most runaways are young, inexperienced suburban kids who run away to major urban areas. . . . They often become the easy victims of street gangs, drug pushers, and hardened criminals. Without adequate food or shelter, they are prey to a whole range of medical ills . . . (p. 365)

National attention on the problems of runaway and homeless youth is, however, a relatively recent phenomenon, according to the National Network of Runaway and Youth Services (1985).[6] Walker[7] reported that there was a marked increase in the number of runaway youth in the 1968 to 1972 period as well as an increased interest by many individuals in helping them. The growing problem of missing youths, according to *U.S. News and World Report* in September of 1973, "sprang into the news in mid-August with the discovery in Houston that more than two dozen boys–some of whom were runaways–had been murdered . . . "[8]

Many media outlets, policy makers, and concerned groups have become interested in the scope and severity of the problems of runaway and homeless youth. Much of this interest has been generated by feature stories on runaways in *Parade, Life, Reader's Digest, The New York Times,* and many other magazines and newspapers. Good Morning America, CBS Sunday Morning, ABC 20/20, Nightline, the USA Network, and many other television and radio programs have carried segments on runaways in the early 1980s, according to the National Network.

In 1970 the U.S. Senate Subcommittee to Investigate Juvenile Delinquency held hearings on the increasing numbers of youth who were fleeing from their homes and who were in danger. In 1972, concerned youth service providers and advocates met in Minnesota and recognized the national scope of the problem, the need for specific types of services for these at-risk youth, and the need for communication among shelters across the country. In September of 1974, Congress enacted and President Ford signed the landmark Juvenile Justice and Delinquency Prevention Act and the Runaway Youth Act. In 1977, as Congress developed a greater understanding of the problem of homeless youth and throwaways, (those who are forced out of their homes), the law was amended as the "Runaway and Homeless Youth Act" (RHYA). This legislation authorized the Department of Health, Education, and Welfare to spend several million dollars for three consecutive years on local services to runaways.

The National Network of Runaway and Youth Services was established as a national, non-profit membership organization, and by 1985 was comprised of more than 500 regional, state, and local youth service agencies providing services to runaway, homeless, and other troubled children and youth. In 1984 the National Network implemented YOUTHNET, a national computerized information-sharing telecommunications system, and also became the administering agency for the National Fund for Runaway Children. According to the National Network report, this fund receives donations from groups and individuals and awards the funds to youth shelter programs that need support.

During 1984, according to the National Network, 23.25 million dollars in funds were appropriated by Congress for the RHYA to support 260 runaway and homeless youth shelters across the nation. A portion of these funds was used to support the National Runaway Switchboard, a toll-free hotline and communication channel which counsels youth who are thinking about running away, provides crisis counseling and referral service to runaway and homeless youth, and arranges contact between the youth and their families. In addition, a portion of the RHYA funds goes toward innovative direct service projects and research directed at special issues and problems.

Many state and local governments fund and support services to runaway and homeless youth. Most shelters are administered by community-based non-profit agencies and receive support from their local United Way, religious groups, foundations, and other private sources.

Staff and volunteers at shelters help runaways, homeless youth, and their families when possible, by being accessible and responsive 24 hours a day, 7 days a week. The shelters provide a safe place for the young people to stay while they receive counseling and support services aimed at reuniting the youth with his/her family or securing the most appropriate long-term living arrangements for the youth.

In addition to crisis intervention services, many shelters across the nation provide other specialized services to youth including drug and alcohol counseling, long-term foster care, transportation, recreation, and work readiness training. Since the 1974 implementation of the federal runaway and homeless youth program, shelters have been providing a combination of comprehensive services to these at-risk youth and, when possible, their families and "have been improving the quality and scope of their services to these troubled young people" (National Network, 1985, p. 6). In addition, community agencies such as Boys Clubs, the Salvation Army, Big/Brothers/Big Sisters, YMCA, YWCA, and others have become actively involved in serving runaway and homeless children and youth.

Although the number of shelters for runaways increased from 140 in 1974 to 525 in 1985,[9] only a fraction of the total runaway population receives shelter care or related services.[10]

DEFINITION

Walker's review of the literature from 1934 through 1974 yielded a wide range of definitions of running away. Of the articles which attempted to define the term "runaway," very few used the same definition. Some of the key elements which Walker found in the definition of the runaway were 1) age of the child, 2) lack of parents' permission or consent, 3) psychological characteristics, 4) inclusion in missing persons records, 5) identification by a juvenile court, 6) child's knowledge about consequences of his/her action, 7) length of time away from home, 8) where the child ran from, 9) where the child ran to, and 10) previous runaway behavior. The most frequently used definition for running away from home requires the youth to be gone without his/her parents' permission or consent for a certain length of time (p. 22).

The National Network report used the following definitions:

"Runaways" are children and youth who are away from home at least overnight without parental or caretaker permission.

"Homeless" are youth who have no parental, substitute, foster, or institutional home. Often these youth have left or been urged to leave with the full knowledge or

approval of legal guardians and have no alternative
home.

"Systems kids" are youth who have been taken into the
custody of the state due to confirmed child abuse and
neglect or other serious family problems. Often these
children have been in a series of foster homes, have had
few opportunities to develop lasting ties with any adult,
are school dropouts, and have few independent living
skills.

"Street kids" are long-term runaway or homeless youth
who have become adept at fending for themselves "on
the street," usually by illegal activities.

"Missing children" can refer to any child whose
whereabouts are unknown. It is most often used to refer
to children who are believed to have been abducted and
victims of foul play and/or exploitation (p. 1).

Gulotta[11] said, "While the term 'runaway' has been applied
in a manner which places the onus of responsibility on the
youngster, it has neglected to give equal attention to parental
abandonment" (p. 549). Gulotta[12] used the term "castaway" to refer
to those youth who did not willingly choose to leave home but "for
whatever reasons were placed out of their homes by the parents and
were then reported by either their parents or the police as runaways"
(p. 544). In 1975 *U. S. News and World Report* noted the seeming
growth in numbers of "push-outs" or "throwaways".[13] These
involuntary runaways were described as young people who were
unwanted in their homes, either before or after running away.

According to the National Network, there is no typical
runaway or homeless youth. They are most often youth between the
ages of 12 and 18. The runaway population is comprised of male,
female, White, Black, Hispanic, Asian, urban and rural youth from
all socio-economic classes, from every state and congressional
district in the nation.

Burke and Burkhead[14] pointed to the varying definitions of
the term "runaway" as one difficulty in integrating the literature
regarding runaway youth. Many who have reviewed the literature
have noted that some studies used this term loosely, and often
provided no operational criteria for running away.[15]   Brennan,

Huizinga and Elliott defined a runaway as a young person between the ages of 12 and 18 who leaves home with the intention of running away, stays away for more than 48 hours without parental permission, and knows that he or she will be missed.[16] The most common criteria for defining runaway youth are that they be 10 to 17 years old and leave home without permission from a parent or guardian at least overnight.[17] Several studies, however, have suggested that the number of times a youth runs away is a critical defining variable.[18] The majority of youth run away only once and may be seeking pleasure or adventure.[19]

More recent studies have suggested that only children who run away more than once should be characterized as exhibiting runaway behavior.[20] Gulotta reported that 84% of runaways in his study were one-time runners who left in response to a problem at home or school. In contrast, Roberts found that one-time runaways had little conflict with their parents and, generally, ran for adventure. He noted, however, that youth who run two or more times utilized running away as a problem-solving method. Roberts also found that repeat runners had more serious problems in all aspects of their lives than one-time runners.[21]

Palenski and Launer[22] did not define runaway behavior in terms of legal definitions or individual motives, but rather viewed the designation of runaway as a social process (p. 347). The young person who runs away was not seen as a child who leaves home but as one who engages in a series of social encounters in which he/she comes to learn the everyday problems and predicaments of living away from home. Runaway behavior, they stated, may or may not be problematic. The process of becoming a runaway was seen as being extremely dependent on the types of encounters a young person has with family, friends, and agents of social control while out of the home.

With regard to the legal status of runaways, in some states they are considered juvenile delinquents and are subject to arrest.[23] If they are picked up by the police, they may be returned home or sent to a reformatory. In other states, running is considered a status offense and is not punishable by detention. These youth are either sent home, referred to a department of social service, or taken to a shelter for runaways.[24]

INCIDENCE / OCCURRENCE / DESCRIPTION

Burke and Burkhead claimed that "the incidence of running away has increased significantly in the last 10 years and is presently considered to be a major social problem" (p. 73). Estimates of the number of runaway and homeless children and youth in America ranged from 1.3 to 2 million each year, and a few studies and extrapolations suggested that there may be as many as 4 million children who run away from home for at least one night each year.[25] Dunford and Brennan reported that Federal Bureau of Investigation statistics indicated that juvenile runaway behavior increased 70% from 1967 to 1972, and that the Baye Senate subcommittee hearings (1973) conservatively estimated that over 1 million children run away in America each year.[26] According to Nye, one youth in 8 will run away, at least overnight, between his/her 10th and 18th birthday.[27] Obtaining exact figures was a problem because parents often did not report that their children are missing.[28]

Walker found the main source available for estimating the number of runaways to be the police arrest and/or missing persons records. Walker reported that these official records had been shown to be low, biased estimates and that other ways of estimating the incidence of runaways on both a local and national level (e.g. household sampling of youth and/or parents, school surveys, telephone surveys, etc.), were being tried. The best estimate frequently quoted in the literature Walker reviewed was that there were about .5 to 1 million youths who ran away from home each year. Based on census data at that time, this would have been approximately 1-1.5% to 3% of the total youth population, ages 10-17, in the United States.

Morgan's study found that 25% of runaways were born to mothers under 18 years of age, 75% came from single parent homes, and 50% had been sexually or physically abused by someone in their household.[29] Hughes reported that a 1987 survey by her organization found that 61% of the teenage youths served in runaway shelters across the U.S. had been abused physically or sexually by parents or other family members.[30]

Morgan[31] also reported that 25% of runaways came from homes where there was alcohol and drug abuse and that within months of running away "2 out of 3 are using drugs regularly (alcohol, marijuana, hash, cocaine, crack and heroin are the most popular), and 2 out of 3 are supporting themselves through prostitution" (p. 257). Other evidence (Opinion Research Corporation, 1976) suggested that runaways were more likely to come from either single-parent or very large families.[32]

Hughes[33] reported that divorced, single-parent, or blended families were far more prone to having a youth reach outside the home for help by running away. Fifty-two percent of youth remained in the county or metropolitan area from which they ran away. Only 12% fit the stereotype of being long-distance runners, and even these may have traveled only 50 to 100 miles from home (p. 65). A 1983 study by Manov and Lowther, cited by Kammer and Schmidt, reported that 52% of runaways traveled less than 10 miles from home, and approximately 70% returned home within one week. About 1 in 20 may be gone for 1 year or longer, and some never return.[34]

Hughes[35] stated:

> Informed professional opinion is that the majority of
> youth who run and are not reported find refuge with
> someone close to them. Street life, respite at a relative's
> or friend's house, or safety in an emergency shelter are
> the primary alternatives for youth on the run (p. 65).

"There are many elements in our society who are aware of the runaways' vulnerability and take advantage of it. We must inject a sense of urgency into the label 'runaway.' It's an uphill battle," said Jay Howell.[36] "Regardless of why the child left, the fact of the matter is that these children are unsophisticated, untrained, inexperienced individuals without a support system or the skills necessary to eke out a decent survival system on the streets of America" (p. 114). Kammer and Schmidt claimed that runaways are at a high risk of becoming victims of violent crime, suffering abuses on the streets, and victimizing others through theft, assault, or drug dealing.[37]

Runaways are difficult to track for conventional demographic and psychological studies, according to Hersch.[38] Kids who come to shelters compose the "typical" sample, but shelters serve less than half of the runaway population and form an inadequate research base. Statistics vary for this reason, but an approximate profile emerged: 36% run from physical and sexual abuse; 44% run from other severe long-term crises such as drug-abusing and/or alcoholic parents or step-family crises; 20% run from short-term crises such as divorce, sickness, death, and school problems (p. 31). Hersch also reported that June Bucy found approximately 70% of runaways who come to emergency shelters have been severely physically abused or sexually molested. Gulotta[39] also reported high incidences of abuse and neglect among runaway youth. And Rader claimed that abusive parental behavior may account for more than one third of all runaway episodes.[40]

Hersch[41] reported that only half of all runaways have a realistic prospect for returning home, often because home continues to be chaotic and parents remain abusive. Foster care placement fails in many cases, and youths run away again and again, increasing their risks of becoming part of the roughly 300,000 children and adolescents who are classified as "hard-core" homeless street kids (p. 31).

A large majority of runaways have severe emotional problems. Hersch[42] cited a 1983 study of adolescents in New York City youth shelters by David Shaffer and Carol L. M. Caton of the New York State Psychiatric Institute which found that "shelter users have a psychiatric profile largely indistinguishable from adolescents attending a psychiatric clinic" (p. 31). Thirty percent were categorized as depressed, 18% as antisocial, and 41% as both depressed and antisocial. Twenty-five percent had attempted suicide and another 25% had contemplated suicide. A 1985 study by the Division of Adolescent Medicine at the Children's Hospital of Los Angeles produced similar findings.[43] Rader said that runaways frequently suffer from emotional problems and learning difficulties and show various antisocial behaviors.[44]

A number of researchers have proposed that recidivism is an important variable in distinguishing between healthy and unhealthy characteristics of runaways.[45] A youth who runs away from home one time may be reacting to a common problem of adolescence in a particular way, while the child who runs away frequently is likely to have more serious problems. Speck, Ginther and Helton found that personality disorders, family disorganization, and delinquency existed only in chronic runaways who belonged in the clinical population and needed professional help.[46] In addition, the American Psychological Association (APA) dropped running away as a diagnostic category in their 1980 revision of the

Diagnostic and Statistical Manual (DSM-III) and included repeated
running away as a diagnostic criterion for conduct disorders in
children and adolescents.[47]

Speck, Ginther and Helton[48] sought to determine whether
there were two separate populations among runaways and to
formulate a model which could predict their status as either first-
time or recidivist. Results of his study did not provide evidence for
either a healthy or unhealthy conception of runaways. The findings,
however, appeared to support indications that first-time runaways
are less healthy than the norms and more healthy than recidivists.
Recidivism received limited support as a factor that discriminated
between the healthy and unhealthy nature of running away, but the
contention that even first-time runaways are healthy adolescents
reacting to common problems in a particular way was not supported
by Speck's research.

Janus, Burgess and McCormack[49] found that the
adolescent male runaways in their study evidenced dramatically
higher rates of sexual and physical abuse than did randomly
sampled populations. These sexually abused runaways responded in
much more highly avoidant patterns coupled with extreme
withdrawal from all types of interpersonal relationships than did
runaways who did not report sexual abuse.

Nye and Edelbrock[50] found that many runaways were from
large, single-parent families with low incomes, but many also came
from average-income, intact families. Rader reported that most
runaways, in fact, were from middle- and upper-class families.[51]
There were equal numbers of boys and girls who ran away, and
about half went alone.[52]

Adams, Gulotta and Clancy said that 74% of the runaways
in their study reported leaving home because they did not get along
with their parents.[53] Poor parent-child relationships and extreme
family conflict were also found from other studies of runaways.[54]
Adams and Munro[55] said that many runaways felt conflict with the
value systems of their parents and a loss of individuality in their
families. They often had poor communication with parents and felt a
lack of warmth, affection, and support from their families. They
perceived their families as cold, not understanding, and indifferent.
The findings of Post and McCoard[56] from 76 adolescent runaways
revealed that their greatest needs were concerned with living
arrangements, family relationships, and communication with

parents. The respondents perceived information about sex, drugs, and alcohol as least important (p. 212).

In her study of a group of 30 runaways and 30 nonrunaways, Spillane-Grieco found that runaways and their parents reported receiving far less empathy and positive regard from each other as compared to the nonrunaways and their parents.[57] She also found[58] that:

> . . . the concern for their children expressed by the parents of the runaways was real. That both the runaways and their parents reported not feeling much care and love from each other appeared to be due more to a lack of effective communication than a lack of genuine feelings of love. Parents were not able to express their affection to the children, and vice versa, the children could not express their affection to the parents. (p. 165)

In the study by Brennan, Huizinga and Elliott[59] poor teacher-student relations and school problems were found to be "causal factors" for adolescents running away, and 75% performed poorly in school. Adams, Gulotta, and Clancy[60] reported that 69% of runaways said t hey were infrequently invited by other students to be included in school activities, and thought their teachers perceived them as "easily frustrated, strong willed, impulsive, and quick-tempered" (p. 720). Eighty-two percent of the runaways in this study viewed themselves as failures and 69% reported feeling useless. Nye and Edelbrock cited research which showed runaways to have serious school problems including truancy, dropping out, pregnancy, alcohol and drug abuse, severe depression, and suicide. They also often performed poorly, exhibited low academic motivation, disliked school, and were labeled as troublemakers.[61] Goldmeier and Dean found that runaways were more likely to be enrolled in vocational and nonacademic programs in school than were nonrunaways. They also found that runaways had poorer grades, less interest in going to college, and more difficulty getting along with teachers and school counselors than did nonrunaways.[62]

In a follow-up study, Olson and his associates[63] demonstrated that in adulthood those who had run away as youths experienced significantly more psychological and social problems than nonrunaways. This study showed that more than half of the runaways dropped out of high school and not one went beyond high school. They had difficulty maintaining regular employment, had poor interpersonal relationships, and more than 50% had been divorced.

Englander's study[64] of 52 runaway and 51 nonrunaway female adolescents suggested that lower-middle-class female runaways were more likely than others "(a) to perceive their parents, perhaps realistically, as relatively lacking in warmth and supportiveness, and (b) to report themselves as relatively high in socially undesirable, self-oriented traits and relatively low in socially desirable, interpersonally oriented traits" (p. 485). Kammer and Schmidt[65] summarized the profile of the runaway as:

> . . . not positive. They feel insecure, unhappy, impulsive, depressed, helpless, lonely, alienated, anxious, self-critical, restless, untrusting, and misunderstood. They see their personal lives as unmanageable, a perception that is borne out to some extent by their unsuccessful interpersonal relationships and poor academic performance (p. 26).

REASONS / PREDISPOSING FACTORS

A number of proposed explanations for runaway behavior of young people exist which appear contradictory, and thereby suggest that our understanding of the behavior is very limited and inconclusive.[66] Much of the literature has focused not on a functional analysis of the phenomenon, but simply on the reasons children give for running away. This focus has hindered the development of a coherent theory of running away.[67]

A number of researchers have noted that running away is not a random occurrence, especially for repeat runaways, but is related to personal and social phenomena.[68] In addition, Blood cautioned researchers not to create scapegoats in the search for explanations of runaway behavior. She suggested that merely blaming families, schools, or the youth themselves is unwarranted.[69]

Burke and Burkhead[70] discerned 3 major perspectives from the early literature on runaway behavior: the psychopathological perspective; the normal-healthy perspective; the sociological perspective.

The psychopathological perspective. The early research on runaway youth came primarily from the psychiatric literature, and the conclusions were based on nonsystematic case studies and clinical observations with only a few youths who were repeat runaways.[71] These early studies, according to Walker, generally reported runaway youth as experiencing severe psychopathology, and followed the traditional model which attributes the basic reasons for running away to problems within the individual child. Runaway youth were characterized as emotionally disturbed, mentally deficient, lacking ego strength, having poor impulse control, and suffering from depression.[72] Jorgensen and his associates[73] found in their analysis of open-ended questionnaires from 292 runaways that over one half responded "depressed" to the statement: "Lately, I've felt . . . "

The psychiatric influence in the early literature culminated in the new diagnostic category, Runaway Reaction, in the 1968 revision of the American Psychiatric Association's Diagnostic and Statistical Manual of Mental Disorders published in 1968 (DSM-II). Youth in this category were described as timid, immature, feeling rejected by their family, having few friends, and exhibiting inadequate problem-solving abilities.[74] They were said to escape threatening situations by running, which ultimately proved to be a self-defeating pattern. This characterization seemed to have fallen out of favor, as evidenced by the deletion of the Runaway Reaction category from the DSM in 1980, the DSM-III.[75]

The normal-healthy perspective. Another predominant theme in the literature has considered running away as a healthy and normal act. Researchers with this perspective have rejected the notion that running away is symptomatic of underlying personality, psychological, family, or social problems.[76] Gutierres and Reich advocated a developmental-motivational perspective in understanding runaway behavior.[77] Children who experience interpersonal relationship difficulties, especially within the family, attempt to resolve those difficulties in a manner which is personally meaningful and relevant.[78] "They get away from the situation by escaping rather than aggression. Their tendency to run away indicates a well-developed coping mechanism" (p. 92).

Walker reported that a small number of studies suggested that running away represents a positive and natural step in the normal growing up process for many youths. In 1975 Chapman, in

Burke and Burkhead, suggested that runaway behavior is merely a daring and courageous, although impulsive, act, and was related neither to delinquency nor to emotional disturbance.[79] Ambrosino reported that running away is a function of normal adolescent development toward independence and autonomy. She believed that this behavior is simply an aspect of transition to adulthood and can be viewed as a positive psychological sign.[80] Neither Chapman nor Ambrosino, however, offered any empirical data to support their conclusion.

There are some empirical studies, however, which do support a normal-healthy perspective. Some researchers who interviewed youths have reported runaway behavior as merely a search for adventure since only a very small number of runaways have serious personal or family problems.[81] Homer also concluded that running away generally is not a cry for help but a search for adventure.[82] From this perspective, the main difference between runaways and other adolescents is their drastic choice of action and their decision to demand greater control of their lives. [83]

Homer viewed the notion that runaways are psychopathic or sociopathic as a myth, and suggested that all runaways can be put into two primary categories: "those running to" and "those running from." She believed that the latter are a small group who are running from family and personal problems and/or are angry with their parents, and who are running to "cool off." The majority of runaways, according to Homer, however, are in the former category and are running to find adventure, pleasure, or new experiences.[84] Sharlin and Mor-Barak,[85] examining female adolescent runaways, found that girls who "run to" were younger, more impulsive, had internal locus of control, and had history of more runaways and longer periods of staying away from home. Girls who "run from" were older, more reflective, had external locus of control, and had history of fewer runaways and shorter periods away from home (p. 387).

Recent research has generally not continued to support the normal-healthy perspective as an adequate explanation.[86] The National Network report stated that "most youth service providers agree that, in the vast majority of cases, the young people are running away from something rather than to something. The mistaken public perception that runaway and homeless youth are on the streets because they are pursuing a carefree and rebellious lifestyle is rapidly dissolving" (p. 2). Jorgenson and his associates analyzed open-ended questionnaires from 292 runaways and suggested that these youth run to escape something with which they can not or will not deal.[87]

Palenski and Laumer[88] viewed running away as a part of conventional adolescent development, a diffuse activity with few concrete boundaries that are easily recognizable (p. 348). Runaway behavior was viewed as not systematically distinct from other adolescent behavior, since it includes the acts of exploring, testing, and defining one's limits.

Brothers[89] presented the Gestalt Theory of healthy aggression in "beyond-control youth", including runaway adolescents (p. 582). From this point of view, human beings, as members of the animal kingdom, use running away as a primary means of coping with danger. Here running is the flight portion of the fight-or-flight response. Running may also be viewed as a form of fight as well as flight, since running may serve as a means of fighting for parental limits, of asking to be stopped. Whether it is fight or flight, the common ground for runaways is a "felt inability to both remain in the family and to structure themselves and the environment into figures that allow and sustain growth" (p. 582).

The sociological perspective. Researchers with a sociological perspective believed that running away is a function of disturbed family life styles.[90] It was suggested that many runaways leave their homes to avoid physical or psychological abuse,[91] and others may have run from the experience of rejection in their homes.[92]

Walker reported that an increasing number of studies, especially during the 1964-1974 period, follow what she termed the "environmental context model," which attributes the reasons for running away to various situational factors outside the individual. Running from family problems is the reason most often given by adolescents themselves in several studies. Runaways reported poor communication with parents, negative labeling by their parents, and long-term conflict within their families.[93] A 12-year follow-up study of runaway children reported that the problems among runaways, particularly in interpersonal relationships, continue into adulthood.[94]

Others have run because they were physically or sexually abused or victims of extreme neglect.[95] In 1977 *U.S. News and*

World Report said, "Young Americans in unprecedented numbers
are running away from their homes to escape a growing epidemic of
once unspeakable crimes–incest and child abuse."[96] The report
pointed out that social workers in some areas said that incest and
other forms of child abuse are cited by 40 to 60 per cent of
teenagers and even younger children as their main reasons for
running away. In their study of runaways who were both physically
and sexually abused Kurtz, Kurtz and Jarvis[97] found that a larger
proportion encountered a wider range of personal problems, came
from multiproblem families, and, in short, were significantly more
vulnerable and much worse off than runaways who only experienced
either physical or sexual abuse (p.555). In addition Kurtz, Kurtz and
Jarvis found that runaways who experienced only physical or sexual
abuse also reported more problems and were at greater risk than
runaways who did not report either type of abuse (p. 555).

In 1975 *U.S. News and World Report* indicated that survey
results showed that recession and inflation have a tremendous effect
on the number of "throwaways" in many areas.[98] In the report
Bohnsack said that:

> . . . the problem of throwaways is growing, especially as
> the recession continues and more parents lose their jobs.
> . . . It gets to the point where parents really don't want to
> take care of them emotionally and certainly not
> financially. So as far as many parents are concerned, if
> the kid gets out of the house and makes it on his own,
> O.K. If he doesn't, then that's got to be O.K., too (p. 49).

Many service providers believed that a high percentage of
these youth run away because their families have become
dysfunctional. That is, the family has such economic, marital,
alcohol and drug abuse or mental health problems that there has
been a total breakdown between the youths and their families
resulting in crisis situations, according to The National Network
report (p.2). Some of these youth are socially and emotionally
troubled. They have experienced a series of other personal failures
with their schools, the law, the job market, drug and alcohol abuse,
and other adolescent situations. They see leaving as their way out.

In Walker's review of the literature, she found one
outstanding fact about reasons for running away which holds up
across most studies. Regardless of their orientation towards
runaways or their sample base, these studies found that runaways

most often have inadequate parent-child relationships and unhappy, stressful home environments.

Fishman said that the middle- or upper-class runaway teenager and one who comes from a background of poverty may not be so different.[99] Both, he reported, perceive their home environments as lacking in basic nurturing and support. Hersch[100] said that "contrary to a lingering perception of runaways as adolescent adventurers, most are victims of dysfunctional families and are fleeing from a stressful environment" (p. 31).

Two sociopsychological theories have been proposed which focus the etiology of running away largely on relationships in family, school, and the peer group. Brennan, Huizinga and Elliott[101] suggested that if three conditions are present, youths are unlikely to engage in deviant behavior, including running away: youths are involved in legitimate, rewarding, and satisfying roles; they feel they are viewed positively by reference groups and have high self-esteem; and, they feel positive about school and community and feel they have reasonable control over their lives. According to this theory, the problems of youth are located in the structures of family and school which may deny such roles, relationships and positive labels to adolescents.

Brennan, Huizinga and Elliott[102] looked within the family and school for the development of positive bonds to provide social controls against deviant behavior, including running away. These bonds are of two types: social integration bonds and personal commitment bonds. Social bonds include such variables as participation in satisfying activities, occupation or rewarding social roles, effective sanctioning networks, and so on. Personal commitment bonds, on the other hand, refer to internalized values and beliefs. They include commitment to conventional norms, positive self-esteem, negative attitudes toward delinquent behavior, and so on (p.30). According to this theory, running away may be the result of initial inadequate social bonds or strains on those bonds which develop during adolescence if the needs are not met within conventional social roles.

Brennan, Huizinga and Elliott[103] integrated the social-psychological strain and control theories to explain runaway behavior. The strain theory hypothesizes that youths who fail to achieve personal needs in the family will run away. From this perspective, running is the result of stress (or strain) in the home and/or problems with parental relationships. The control theory suggests that runaways are those youth whose "early socialization produced weak commitments to conventional norms and low levels of integration into social groups" (p. 64) and, therefore, are not controlled by social expectations.

A more recent study examined the extent to which stressful life events and methods of coping with stress led to runaway behavior.[104] The incidents precipitating a runaway event, reported by the youths, included physical punishment, parents' alcohol problems, and parents' reactions to school and divorce. The most immediate precipitating factor was angry outbursts by parents which often included the parents making negative statements about the child. Roberts[105] defined methods of coping used by young people to solve problems. He reported that the majority of runaway youth (83%) said they attempted to solve personal problems by taking drugs or alcohol, leaving the house, crying, attempting suicide, going to sleep, or running away. Fors and Rojek[106] found that drug use and abuse is two to three times more prevalent for runaways than for youths who were in school (p. 13). On the other hand, according to Roberts[107], nonrunaways said they coped with stressful situations by evaluating the possible solutions to problems and considering the possible consequences of their behavior prior to taking action.

One other theoretical perspective can be noted: the problem behavior proneness theory of Jessor and Jessor.[108] They looked within the individual for the development of conventional attitudes and values on the one hand and for tolerant attitudes toward deviance and values easily developed through deviant behavior on the other. In the social environment they looked for the level of support and controls favorable to conventional behavior versus approval and models for deviant behavior.

Nye[109] recognized that all these theories which attempt to explain runaway behavior have something to contribute. He claimed, however, that theories which explain runaway behavior as a function of individual psychopathology cannot explain why some youths having characteristics such as poor impulse control, mental deficiency, emotional disturbance, or a lack of ego strength run away, and others do not. He further maintained that theories within a sociological perspective are neither able to explain why those youth (about 20%) who have good family and school relationships still run, nor why those who have conflicted and alienated relationships in the family and/or school but do not run (p. 277).

Nye[110] drew upon concepts in both psychology and economics to develop his theory of choice and exchange. A basic assumption of this perspective is that humans seek rewards and avoid costs to obtain the best outcomes from among those choices which may be available to them. Rewards include anything–relationships, experiences, positions, or feeling–that is positively valued. Costs are anything that the person would prefer to avoid, including opportunities passed because time or resources are preempted which otherwise might be used to pursue other rewards. Outcomes are the balance of rewards minus costs (p. 278).

Nye[111] described the functioning of family, school, and the peer group to help explain runaway behavior and recidivism in running away. The school, parents, and the peer group serve as both costs and rewards in the lives of adolescents. According to Nye, school exacts costs from adolescents in terms of their time from Monday through Friday, time which, if it were not for school, could be available for pursuing jobs, traveling, or other potentially rewarding activities. To many young people, much of the high school curriculum is uninteresting, and the boredom and stress involved are part of the costs. On the other hand, school can also be rewarding. Many young people view education as necessary for success in their eventual chosen field of work, which can in turn be expected to support their chosen life style. Students who like school are receiving important rewards which compensate for the costs of their time and sacrifice of other pursuits. For those who do not like school and do not do well academically or in school related activities, rewards are not experienced. Those young people experience costs from school which outweigh any of its rewards. Such costs often include being labeled as dumb and/or lazy, and these students may choose more and more to engage in other activities which further decrease the rewards and increase the costs they receive in school. Running away can be expected to provide opportunities to gain rewards and to eliminate the costs which they experience in school.

Parents, according to Nye,[112] can exact heavy costs from children in terms of the rules which they devise for family members. Such rules may involve not only the carrying out of household tasks but also may include restrictions on the children's autonomy in such areas as diet, dress, activities, and other behaviors which parents typically attempt to limit. Parents usually supply rewards as well including food, shelter, approval, security, and love. In childhood,

Nye said, parents may maintain an appropriate balance of costs and rewards for their children, or the rewards may exceed the costs. As children move into their adolescent years, however, they develop new interests and may wish to experiment with drugs, alcohol, and/or sexual activity; they may even want to get a job or quit school. There are many activities which adolescents wish to explore which parents typically attempt to limit or prohibit. Conflicts between parents and adolescents may become chronic, and youths may see the costs of remaining with the family as outweighing the rewards. Parents as well may feel their own rewards would be greater without the costs of adolescent care.

The peer group is a great source of both costs and rewards for adolescents, according to Nye.[113] The successful scholar or athlete receives rewards of prestige and approval and has many social opportunities available. The young person who is physically unattractive or is failing academically may feel the costs of being socially isolated and shamed. Friendship groups ordinarily provide approval and companionship. They are usually based on similar values and tastes and serve as a buffer against social disapproval in the larger school community by disputing the legitimacy of societal values and norms.

Any group exacts some costs, even though friendship groups offer more rewards. Members of a group must perform in ways that earn group acceptance and approval. In a conforming group, this tends to constrain the individual to achievement in school and restrain delinquent behavior, including running away from home. Groups which are oriented to delinquent activities influence individuals toward more deviant behavior and toward rejecting conventional commitments to school and family. Either way, they offer approval and models for behavior. Nye[114] developed a series of 18 hypotheses in 3 general categories with regard to runaway behavior: running for better outcomes; societal-level variation; and consequences of running (p. 284). Included in the area of running for better outcomes are his first 4 hypotheses which view running as increasing rewards. These hypotheses are relative to the group which Nye categorized as "positive runaways", about 20%of runaways:

> 1) Running does occur among youths who have and
> perceive that they have good relationships with family,
> school, and friends.

2) Youths who place a high value on independence
relative to value on school achievement are more likely
to run than are those with the opposite value hierarchy.

3) Among youths with good family, school, and peer
relationships, those who value independence highly are
more likely to run than those who value it less.

4) Among youths who have good relationships in
family, school, and peer groups, those who have an
idealized picture of the world "out there" are more likely
to run than are those who perceive it realistically (pp.
284-285).

Nye's next 3 hypotheses have to do with running to reduce
costs, and are related to his category of runaways (about 75%) who
are unhappy about one or more of the major components in their
lives:

5) Among youths who feel rejected by parents and
school, those who feel the road offers fewer costs than
home are likely to run.

6) Close peer relationships increase the likelihood of
running if the peer group is delinquent, and decrease it if
the peer group is conforming.

7) Other conditions being constant, youths who are
dissatisfied with family and school are more likely to run
if they anticipate sorrow and anxiety on the part of
parents and teachers (pp. 287-288).

Nye continued that this category of runaways is very
diverse. While all of these youths seek to reduce costs, the nature
and severity of costs differ greatly. These youths have their own
ideas about what costs are important and unimportant. Many also
are unrealistic concerning the costs and rewards to be found on the
road, while others are correct in believing that their outcomes will
be better by leaving home.

The category which he labeled "pushouts", Nye suggested,
might well be omitted from the study of runaways per se, because
their departure is usually not against the will of the parent. He cited

other research which suggested that this group constitutes approximately 5% of youths who are out of their homes.

With regard to societal-level variation, Nye believed that choice and exchange theory suggests that rates should vary because, as the beliefs and attitudes about running and societal responses to it vary, increased or decreased rewards and costs accrue to runaways. He offered the next 5 hypotheses in this area:

8) If running behavior is decriminalized in a society, more adolescents will run and fewer will return to their families.

9) If the runaway episodes are attributed to deviant parental behavior, runaway rates will be higher than if the causes of running are attributed to youths.

10) As a society provides more shelter, food, protection, and other resources for runaways, the rate of running will increase.

11) As the proportion of single-parent and reconstructed families increases in a society, the rate of running from families will increase.

12) As societies reduce parent-child and school-child conflict and alienation, runaway rates will decline (pp. 292-293).

Nye noted that runaways and professionals who serve them report both negative and positive consequences to running away but that research on the consequences for individuals is fragmentary (p. 293). He offered his last six hypotheses as ones which might be tested by research.

13) Youths from average family and school situations who run because of an ideal image of life "out there" are likely to be better satisfied with their families and schools as a consequence of the run.

14) Youths who leave home because of lack of opportunity for educational and vocational training who support themselves in legitimate activity will accomplish more and be better satisfied with their

accomplishments than would be youths of equal ability
who do not run.

15) Youth victims of abuse and persecution by parents
through no fault of their own are likely to improve their
situations by running.

16) Runaways who support themselves partly or wholly
by illegitimate activities are likely to experience poorer
long-term outcomes than are equivalent youths who did
not run.

17) Highly delinquent, truant pushouts who leave home
are likely to achieve better outcomes than are those who
remain at home provided they receive extended therapy
and a sufficiently structured living situation to
discourage deviant behavior.

18) Delinquent behavior is increased in a society as the
result of adolescent runaway behavior and, by running
away from home, youths are more likely to engage in
delinquent behavior than if they had stayed home (pp.
294-296).

Hughes[115] wrote that "It's a myth that teenagers run away
from home to seek adventure or to find themselves. Youth today
know the dangers of the streets. In most cases, they run away to
survive abuses occurring at home or family conflicts that feel
unbearable" (p.64). He claimed, "There is no disagreement about
the significance of the family environment to runaway behavior" (p.
65).

Hughes[116] believed that the reasons for running away are
best spoken by the youths themselves. Maureen (age 18), as
reported by Hughes, said, "I was a runaway for 4 years because no
one cared for me and because people kept putting me in group
homes and institutions, when all I needed was someone to love and
care about me" (p. 64).

Becky (age 17) said, "I was abused by my father for years.
I had no one to turn to. I thought I had a 50-50 chance on the streets,
but no chance at home" (p. 64).

James (age 16) said, "My father just totally ignored me
after he got married again. He acted like I was a buddy to him, like

he just didn't want me around. One day, we had an argument and he told me I could just leave, so I did" (p. 64).

Easton has been quoted by Berman[117] as stating that "We're finding that the majority run away because of such things as curfews, arguments with their parents about clothes and music, arguments over friends, worry about a bad report card and a variety of other issues" (p.114).

According to Ruffino, in Berman,[118] "A breakdown of communication is at the heart of the matter. Most parents aren't bad parents, and most kids aren't bad kids. They just don't know how to talk and listen to one another" (p. 114). Kammer[119] said that running is motivated by many complex factors, but that family conflict and stress in school often precipitate the run.

Comer[120] wrote that:

> . . . there is no single cause, nor is running away always a sign of mental disorder. On the contrary, a child who runs away from inhumane treatments is demonstrating good judgement or sound psychological health. Most children experience the impulse to run away at some point when parents are setting limits or denying wishes. Many children simply "run away" to a neighbor or relative for a few hours or a day, often returning just before dinner or bedtime. These behaviors are due to the normal struggle for emotional separation and independence, not pathological illness (p. 146).

Comer continued:

> Serious running away is often due to physical or emotional disorder—in the family, the environment, or the child—early and intense struggles for power and control between parent and child are often an underlying factor. Drug and sexual abuse, violence, and other conditions between parents that create strong negative and inconsistent feelings in their children can lead to runaway behavior. Tensions related to divorce, remarriage, and family moves may also create conditions that encourage a child to run away from home (p. 146).

Brennan, Huizinga and Elliott,[121] in their study of runaways and nonrunaways, reported that all 47 runaway participants in the study said that they received less support from their fathers than from their mothers. The runaways reported more punishment and less support from parents than nonrunaways. Results of their study indicated a relationship between the sex of the youth and parental control. Runaway girls reported the most control, and runaway boys reported the least control by parents.

Blood and D'Angelo, in their study of runaways and nonrunaways, found that a higher proportion of runaways consistently label their issues as major.[122] Runaways perceive more intensity of conflict with their parents, and conflict on a broader range of issues. According to Gottlieb and Chafetz, most parent-child confrontations leading to runaway behavior are provoked by differences that both generations see as unresolvable.[123] They also reported that parent-child differences are seldom eliminated when the child and parents attempt reconciliation.

TYPOLOGIES / CLASSIFICATION SYSTEMS

Many of the articles which Walker reviewed discussed runaways and their behavior or motives according to a variety of conditions and descriptive variables. Some of the most frequent comparisons among runaways and between runaways and nonrunaways were made according to the variables which include sex, ethnicity, age, family background, number of times running away (once vs. repeater), reason for running away, severity of problems, juvenile delinquency record, or school grades and record.

Walker defined these classifications as "basically heuristic devices for explaining differences in runaway behavior" (p. 24). She observed that the majority of these systems had been developed from observations and inferences about runaway behavior accumulated in therapy and counseling cases of the respective investigators. Most of the systems referred to the psychological reasons or motives underlying a youth's runaway behavior. Several schemes were developed from a classical psychoanalytic perspective, and most, according to Walker, employed a very narrow and limited set of variables to delineate the runaway and his/her behavior.

In contrast to the vaguely defined and theoretically derived systems were the empirical typologies of runaway behavior developed by Brennan, Huizinga and Elliott.[124] Walker reported that these were the only classification systems which were derived from a large set of psychological, sociological, and demographic variables, and were based on a sound set of rather sophisticated multivariate statistical methods developed for generating typologies from empirical sets of data. Walker said that even though these typologies overcame many problems associated with the other systems she reviewed, "the meaning and possible uses of the individual types need to be clarified and refined, and the typologies must be further validated and developed" (p. 30). Of the classification schemes Walker reviewed she stated that "none of them at present reflects a conceptual framework broad enough to consider or describe a wide range of runaways" (p. 30).

Greene and Esselstyn, reported in Roberts,[125] described 3 types of runaway girls as the "rootless," the "anxious," and the "terrified." Their "rootless runaway" has parents who probably lavished her with praise as a child and never set limits. She may have dropped out of school, used drugs, and quit a series of jobs. Her parents then became frightened and began to set limits. The girl, a pleasure seeker who often requires immediate gratification, runs away. She may return home, have her way for a while, and then run again when her parents again impose limits.

Reported in Roberts,[126] Green and Esselstyn's "anxious runaway" is one who is frequently from a multi-problem family. She may have to help with younger siblings, household chores, and family finances. Her father, if at home, may drink heavily and may physically and/or verbally abuse her. She becomes anxious and runs to find someone to talk to or to seek help for herself or the family, but is glad to return home. Their "terrified runaway" runs from her father's or step-father's sexual advances toward her. She may often invite friends to visit her at home, or stay away as often as she can to avoid being alone with her sexually abusive father.

English[127] proposed a 4-tiered system of classification for runaways which consists of "floaters," "runaways," "splitters," and "hard road freaks." He defined "floaters" as youths who test the idea of running away by talking about it in order to relieve family tensions, and who then usually change their minds and do not run. If they actually do run, they return home within 48 hours. Those he called "runaways" include youth who leave a destructive family situation, those who hope to call attention to a situation and thereby bring help, and those who run from fear of, or discovery of, a problem (such as an unwanted pregnancy) which they consider

unsharable. Those whom English designated as "splitters" are those
who run because of minor frustrations and whose peers perceive
running away as positive. The "hard road freaks" are generally older
youth, usually 17-20 years of age, who have broken ties with their
families and live a nomadic life-style.

Stierlin[128] identified 4 types of runaways: 1) abortive, 2)
lonely schizoid, 3) crisis, and 4) casual. The abortive and lonely
schizoid runaways are unsuccessful, the casual ones are successful,
and the crisis runaways are partially successful. Runaway success
was defined as the "achievement of geographical distance and/or
premature independence" (p. 57). Stierlin looked at the family
dynamics of runaways and explained transactional modes "which
reflect interplay and/or relative dominance of centripetal and
centrifugal pushes and pulls between the generations" and "operate
as the covert organizaing transactional background to the more
overt and specific child-parent interactions" (p. 58).

According to Stierlin's[129] hypotheses, the runaway types
relate in certain ways to three transactional modes. Under the
binding mode, the child is locked into a parental orbit from which
he does not run away or makes an abortive attempt to do so. All of
these runaways, including the lonely schizoid type, tend to avoid
peers. Under the expelling mode, the child is neglected and
abandoned by his parents which results in early and casual
runaways who adapt well to the runaway culture. Under the
delegating mode, a blend of the binding and expelling modes, a
child is encouraged by his parents to move out from them up to a
point at which they exert control. These youth often run away in a
crisis situation and experience conflicts of missions and conflicts of
loyalties.

Dunford and Brennan[130] developed a taxonomy of
runaway youth based on interviews conducted with fifty-three
runaways as they were being admitted into a runaway facility.
Descriptions of the six runaway types were based upon results from
runaways' scores on standardized measurement scales. The scales
were selected or developed to measure variables known to be
associated with runaway behavior and included runaways'
relationships with parents, their grades in school, level of self-
esteem, peer group influences, and drug use. The Dunford and
Brennan taxonomy can be summarized as follows:

Type 1–Self-confident and unrestrained runaway girls. This
type was comprised only of girls who had poor parental relations.

Low levels of discipline by parents and high levels of unsupervised freedom described this runaway type. Girls in this group achieved high grades and showed high levels of self-esteem and positive attitudes towards teachers and peers.

Type 2–Well-adjusted runaway youth. These runaways did not perceive excessive control or punishment from their parents. They felt positive about school and showed high scores on measures of self-esteem. They had the lowest level of negative peer group influence and reported very low levels of drug use.

Type 3–Double-failure. high delinquency involvement: Youth in this group showed high levels of involvement in delinquent activities as well as poor relationships at home and poor grades in school. They experienced a high level of parental rejection and few parental achievement expectations or rewards. They reported high levels of peer and teacher negative labeling.

Type 4–Fleeing youth. Fleeing youth represented the oldest group profiled, having a mean age of 15.2 years. Youth in this group were of high socioeconomic status and reported experiencing excessive control and exceedingly high demands for achievement by their parents. They were deprived of privileges, perceived a high level of parental rejection, and had low self-esteem scores.

Type 5–Young, highly regulated, and negatively influenced youth. This was the youngest group profiled, having a mean age of 12.1 years. These youth reported having good relationships with their parents. They reported, however, that their parents exercised high levels of control over them and used physical punishment frequently. They also reported experiencing high achievement demands from their parents, low self-esteem, and high levels of negative peer group influences.

Type 6–Young and unrestrained youth. These youth came from low socioeconomic backgrounds and experienced very low levels of parental control and discipline. This group reported low levels of parental demands and relatively high involvement in delinquent activities, including drug use.

From a sociological perspective Brennan, Huizinga and Elliott[131] used results from extensive interviews with runaways to gather data regarding family relationships, peer relations, academic achievement, personal characteristics, beliefs and attitudes, delinquent behavior, and behavioral descriptions of their most recent runaway incidents to support their typology of runaway youth. Class I runaways were described as youth who are neither highly delinquent nor alienated. This group was described as feeling powerless and socially estranged, yet demonstrating a positive self-esteem and having non-delinquent friends. Their running may have been related to social-psychological strain or stress in the home. Class II included delinquent, alienated runaways. This group has serious conflicts with parents, feels rejected, are highly delinquent, have serious problems in school, and have low self-esteem.

Nye[132] described 3 general types of runaways which he drew from research and program literature; positive runaways, runaways who are unhappy about one or more of the major components in their lives, and youths who are abandoned or expelled from home.

The first group is composed of those for whom positive elements are dominant, such as the search for adventure or the opportunity to meet new people, see new places, and to have new experiences. There may be some negative elements, however, in their families, schools, and communities, but these runaways are essentially "positive." It is not that they are running from a bad situation, but they think that things may be more exciting and rewarding down the road.

Nye's second group of runaways are those who have experienced conflict with and alienation from parents, who feel rejected at school, and who often have few peer relationships or are involved with delinquent peer groups. For this group of runaways the dominant motivation for running is to leave a place and relationships about which they have negative feelings.

The third type which Nye described are youths who have essentially been told to leave home. Parents may actually force the child to leave and may even move while the child is gone and leave no indication where they had gone. In other instances the child may have been continually beaten and degraded in ways that made clear that the parents did not value the child and would like the child to leave.

Roberts[133] conducted an in-depth qualitative study of 30 runaways and 30 nonrunaways and found several commonalities among the runaways: family related problems; school failure as evidenced by failing grades, truancy, and suspension; and, frequently, drug and/or alcohol abuse. Twenty-two parents, 10 of runaways and 12 or nonrunaways, were also included in the study. A review of each runaway's family, school, and drug problems led to the development of a parent-youth conflict continuum based on a 5-point scale which is summarized as follows:

Zero to One Level–The Nonrunaway. This is a level of minimal conflict between parent and adolescent, and whatever conflict does occur is tolerated and resolved without the youth's running away. Appropriate compromises between adolescent and parent are sucessfully negotiated.

Level 1+–The Runaway Explorers and Runaway Social Pleasure Seekers. Runaway explorers have a desire to travel alone, or perhaps with a friend, to find adventure and assert their independence. These youths usually inform their parents of their intentions to travel but have not received parental permission. They usually telephone their parents after they have been gone a day or two to allay the parents' fears. If they have not been picked up and returned home by police, Level 1 runaway explorers generally contact their parents voluntarily and ask to return home when they have seen and done what they wanted to do.

Social Pleasure Seekers are usually girls who have had a conflict with their parents over what to them is a major issue, such as a curfew or a restriction on dating a certain boy. Often a relatively good relationship exists between these youths and their parents, but on one particular issue the girls are determined to have their own way. Girls in this group generally sneak out of the house or leave under the pretext of visiting a friend, and then engage in the activity their parents have forbidden. Later they sneak back home or stay at a friend's home and phone their parents to explain and ask to come home. Youths described as Pleasure Seekers are away from home at least 24 hours, but Roberts found similar situations with youths missing from home less than 24 hours and therefore not considered runaways.

Depending on how the family deals with the first runaway episode and future areas of conflict, the runaway behavior may become more frequent and the youth becomes a Level 2 runaway.

Level 2+–Runaway Manipulators. At this level there is more frequent and ongoing conflict between teen and parent over many facets of parental treatment. Youths perceive that siblings and friends are treated better than they are. Running away is an attempt by the adolescent to manipulate the home situation in the hope that, by their running away, the parents will worry and will accept them back on their own terms. These youths generally come from intact homes and their school grades are above average.

Level 3+–Runaway Retreatists. Runaways at this level are those who run from a more heated conflict and tense situation than those at level 2. There are frequent arguments in which parents yell and occasionally hit the youth. Over half the Runaway Retreatists are from "broken homes" (p. 394), and the majority experience failure in school and have been suspended or retained. The retreatist behavior pattern is exhibited by getting drunk or high on drugs almost daily prior to running away.

Level 4+–Endangered Runaways. Eight of the 30 runaways in Roberts' study were at this level. These runaways experience habitual conflicts with parents which result in their being repeatedly physically and/or sexually abused, often while the parent or step-parent is drunk. In most cases there is an alcoholic or recovering alcoholic parent in the home; half of the youths also have a drinking problem. All of them use either amphetamines, acid, cocaine, and/or mescaline regularly. When these youths run away from home it is often because of a recent beating or the threat of being beaten for some misbehavior, real or imagined.

RECOMMENDATIONS FOR
PREVENTION AND TREATMENT

Walker found little across the 42 years of runaway literature she reviewed which addressed the issue of which services or treatments work best for runaways. In most of the articles which addressed it at all, treatment was only a secondary focus. The few themes regarding approaches for dealing with runaways that did emerge from Walker's review were:

1) Running away should not be a police or juvenile court problem but rather a family problem which should be resolved within the family with the help of social service agencies.

2) Counseling and other services for families, especially those in crisis, need to be available. One investigation suggested 24-hour emergency support.

3) Treatment of the runaway should include the family and/or parents, if possible.

4)   With respect to individual therapy with some
runaways, consistent, fair, and warm, supportive
treatment seems to work best.

5) In addition to the option of youth returning home
after running away, adequate alternative services need to
be available.

6) There is some relationship, although complex and
difficult to precisely describe, between institutional
policies and runaway behavior (p. 30).

The 1985 National Network of Runaway and Youth
Services publication entitled "To Whom Do They Belong?" cited a
1985 survey by the Department of Health and Human Services.
Since many homeless youth have fled from abuse, neglect, or other
serious family problems, only about 50% of runaway and homeless
youth have a realistic prospect of returning home or going to a foster
care family (p.3).
       The National Network's response to the question "To whom
do they belong?" was, first, that the question itself is rhetorical.

The blunt fact is that these children and youth belong to
all of us, i.e. if the necessary family support, shelter, and
other services are not available for these youth, our
society will only incur a greater economic liability in
terms of paying for the welfare, institutional, law
enforcement, adult homeless, mental health, and other
inescapable services and programs (p.25).

The National Network's belief was that these youth are best served
by community-based shelters and youth programs which provide a
mix of counseling and other support services in an environment
where the youth feel safe.
       Hughes[134] wrote:

More and more runaway and homeless youth every year
are finding their way to emergency shelters. These
resources are unquestionably the safest and most
constructive available to the youth, their families, and
our communities. The shelters that have 24-hour walk-in
access and a range of counseling and support services are
the most effective because they have been designed to

address the specific needs of this population. . . . The
goal of programs for runaway youth is to reunify
families. There is a strong emphasis on involving the
family and working toward a positive resolution of
conflicts that triggered the youth's flight (p. 66).

Comer[135] said:

There are far too few shelters and youth-protection
programs. Treatment programs for runaways and their
families are often understaffed, and the staffs they have
are overworked. There are even fewer programs for
independent living for older teens who cannot return to
their families. And runaways, because they often have
unique problems, are difficult to help through traditional
clinical therapy programs (p. 146).

Comer continued to state "The best prevention is good child
rearing techniques" (p. 146).

Hersch[136] claimed that many runaways have serious
mental health problems and may suffer neurophysiological
impairment due to drug use. Many shelter program directors believe
that any kid on the street for a month will have to turn to
prostitution and will become increasingly at risk for AIDS. Many
runaway youth need ongoing intensive therapy and/or medical
attention but seldom get it. Shelters are set up to keep the youth for
no more than 15 days. Hersch said that "almost none of the country's
shelters for runaways have on-site medical facilities" (p. 37).

Marcia Quackenbush was quoted by Hersch[137] as saying
that activities that increase the risk of AIDS "are not the special
province of 'bad kids', troubled youth, or the emotionally disturbed"
(p. 34). She believed that education about AIDS prevention must
become a standard part of youth-directed community service.

Janus, Burgess and McCormack[138] suggested that, due to
the high rate of sexual abuse found in their study of male runaways,
questions directly applicable to the experience of sexual abuse be
made part of diagnostic protocols. They believed that clinicians and
others who work with male runaways should be alert to "the likely
possibility of unreported sexual abuse and to the possibility that a
youth's resistance to taking responsibility for resolving the runaway
crises might well be directly related to unreported and untreated
sexual abuse" (p. 414).

The   occurrence   of such high   rates of both sexual and physical   abuse which Janus, Burgess and McCormack[139] found in their   study led   them to believe that   the task of the runaway   shelter is   far more complex than is usually believed. A runaway event may not be a short-term crisis, but   instead may well   be the manifestation of a   potentially   serious trauma   that could   require more serious clinical and social consideration.

In a 12-year follow-up study of runaways ages 10 to 17, Olson,   Liebow,   Mannino and   Shore[140] found that one-time runaways were indistinguishable from their siblings and that chronic problems at school occurred much more frequently with repeat runaways. These findings suggested that   intervention   needs to occur as early   as possible, especially   at the time of the first runaway episode.

Nye[141] suggested   that runaways attend schools with enrollments of 50 to 100 where smaller classes for runaways could provide increased   individual attention which   might   prove   helpful. But Kammer and   Schmidt[142] believed   such a transformation   in most   metropolitan school settings is unlikely to occur.

Kammer   and   Schmidt[143] expressed the   belief   that resources which can counter the runaway's alienation, distrust, and depression with flexibility and understanding must be   within the immediate reach of school counselors. They offered guidelines for counselors in the areas of personal counseling, use of peer listeners, development of support groups, and personal referral. Kammer and Schmidt   believed that a personal   relationship with   an   involved school counselor "may mean the difference between dropping out or remaining in school for the potential runaway" (p. 26). They felt that the effect of such a relationship cannot be overemphasized. Just the recognition of the potential runaway's negative family and school experiences may allay   the sense   of alienation from   the school environment which he or she feels.

Counselors   can   actively   participate in the therapy   process of   runaways who are in   shelters, according to Kammer and Schmidt.[144] They can work to promote discussion of ways in which school issues may   be playing a role in   the family's difficulties and to ensure a supportive network with the school. Runaways frequently use academic failure as a retaliatory tool against their parents. The school   counselor   can   promote   conflict resolution   regarding academic issues for both the   runaways and their parents.

The school counselor can help create a connection between runaways and potential runaways and the school through the development of a strong peer listener program. Goldmeier and Dean[145] found that runaways get along well with their peers, and suggested peer counseling as well. Because a difference in the future adjustment of one-time runaways and repeat runaways has been demonstrated,[146] the school counselor could pair the one-time runaway with a supportive peer listener who has had some training in basic listening skills. The peer listener could gain the trust of peers who may be contemplating running away and perhaps lessen their feelings of rejection and alienation which may preclude their running. The peer listener could also provide information about resources for help.

School counselors can also establish in-school support groups for students who may be having a variety of difficulties. Such groups, according to Kammer and Schmidt,[147] can promote a sense of belonging and teach positive coping skills, both of which can be a powerful deterrent to running. For those who are returning to school and family after a runaway episode, a support group can offer an opportunity for developing positive connections during the transition back into school.

Kammer and Schmidt[148] believed that perhaps the greatest failure of professionals who encounter troubled youth is not making proper and timely referrals to community resource agencies for additional help (p. 27). The school counselor "must not only be aware of facilities for runaways and other agencies which are available to serve youth, but should have personal contact with such service providers so they may lay the groundwork for later involvement" in case coordination for runaways" (p. 27). Kammer and Schmidt said that school counselors can actively help runaway adolescents. Greater awareness, program development, and coordination with community resources are, they believed, first steps in helping these youth.

From the discussion of the theory of healthy aggression in beyond-control youth, Brothers[149] suggested that key aspects of helping these young people include:

> insisting on taking the world apart for them for awhile, that is selecting and limiting what they may and may not contact and do. Second, it is important to provide or allow opportunities for healthy aggression, that is,

interesting and complex situations for them to handle.
Third, it is helpful to encourage these young people to
practice analyzing or taking apart these situations (p.
583).

Brothers also suggested that family therapy can help parents
establish and enforce limits for the child's behavior.

Loeb, Burke and Boglarsky[150] believed that runaways
need to develop a clearer sense of self and an improved facility in
interpersonal relationships. They suggested that the treatment of
runaways should include their being exposed to values clarification
exercises and role-playing exercises aimed at better understanding
others' points of view. As described by Wolk and Brandon,[151] this
training in Rogerian listening skills (empathy, understanding,
positive regard) should be done with the runaway's peers and be led
by counselors who can function as "parent surrogates" (p. 928).

In their study, Loeb, Burke and Boglarsky[152] also found
that runaways, in thinking about their own future families,
anticipated being very different with their children than their parents
had been with them. As a result of this finding the authors suggested
runaways may benefit from specific training in parenting skills and
the opportunity to use these skills in some semi-structured contacts
with young children. These authors also pointed out a need for better
public understanding of the valuable services which runaway
shelters can provide.

Adams, Gulotta and Clancy[153] claimed that the findings of
their study have "strong implications for secondary prevention" (p.
723). They believed that social service personnel need to work with
the total family to reduce communication problems, parent-child
conflict, and stress. Training programs for working with "difficult
adolescents" are much needed. According to Adams, Gulotta and
Clancy, runaways could profit from "being introduced to positive
peer counseling and social competence and friendship initiation
training. Reduced peer problems could help ease some of the stress
that is apparent in the home" (p. 273). Roberts[154] suggested
teaching runaways specific coping skills which might include
training in desired competencies, developing self-confidence and
self-esteem, and appropriate assertiveness techniques.

From her study, Spilane-Grieco[155] suggested the following
practice implications:

1) runaway behavior be approached by the practitioner
as a family-systems problem;

2) every effort should be made to include both parents in
treatment with the runaway;

3) effective communication skills should be a focus of
treatment, with a special emphasis on communicating
positive statements;

4) the development of empathic understanding should
also be a focus of treatment (p. 166).

Stierlin[156] concluded that treatment of runaway youth must
focus on the family and understand the parents' concerns, problems,
and attitudes. Depending on which transactional mode is dominant–
binding, expelling, or delegating–runaways and their families need
to be viewed and treated differently. With runaways who come from
a binding mode, the main task of therapy/treatment with the
adolescent and the family is to unbind them, "to help loosen the
psychological ties which keep the family members in bondage."[157]
Adolescents who run away from the expelling mode need to be held
back by experiencing care and concern within the family, including
the setting of limits, which will help them develop bonds of loyalty.
Where runaways are mainly delegated, the therapeutic task is one
of reconciliation of conflicts and of obligations within the family.

SUGGESTIONS FOR FUTURE
RESEARCH AND EVALUATION

A broad range of recommendations for future research and
evaluation were presented in the literature. In order to reduce the
gaps and inconsistencies which existed in the literature, Walker
made the following suggestions for future studies on runaway youth:

1) Develop a definition (or classification system) for
runaways, if possible, and encourage its use for all future
program descriptions and research or evaluation studies.
At a minimum in the interim, include a clear definition
of the runaway.

2)   Encourage the use of valid social science methodologies (i.e., adequately defined control groups, advanced statistical techniques where appropriate, complete explanations of procedures) in future research and evaluation activities.

3)   Encourage interdisciplinary teams to study runaway youth in order to foster the maximum integration of the various disparate views on treating and understanding runaway youth.

4)   Encourage thoughtful research activities which investigate the predisposing factors and dynamics, especially those related to the parents and family which result in youth running away from home. Because of inconclusive evidence for explaining why youth run away within a single theoretical context, adopt a relatively open-minded position which recognizes the importance of both internal and external factors in explaining runaway behavior.

5)   Encourage systematic and thoughtful research and evaluation activities to examine what services or treatments work best for which type of runaways. Even though there are some recommendations for what should exist and some descriptions of what does exist, there is no evaluative information on what works best.

6)   At all times conduct research and evaluation in a manner which recognizes and respects the rights and needs of runaway youth (pp 33-34).

The National Statistical Survey on Runaway Youth, conducted by the Opinion Research Corporation in 1976, provided a general factual foundation for describing runaway youth, and considerable information concerning motivations for running. Nye[158] suggested that another survey in 1981, repeating many of the same questions would provide important trend data, information concerning the use of programs for runaways, and new characteristics of running and runaways which might have developed in the intervening 5 years. Both the original survey and the proposed new one, according, could provide much more understanding of runaways than had been accomplished up to that time. He suggested that a new survey could also provide an adequate description and evaluation of services provided by runaway shelters.

Nye[159] pointed to research which leaves no doubt about the importance of conflict and alienation among adolescents and their parents and school. He suggested that much of future research relevant to runaways might best be focused on the sources of such conflict and alienation. Findings from such research, according to Nye, would also be relevant to related truancy, juvenile delinquency, and alcohol and drug abuse, since a substantial relationship exists among them.

Nye[160] also pointed out that the husband-wife relationship appeared to have a considerable effect on running away as rates were much higher in single-parent families and in conflicted families. He suggested that research efforts directed toward methods of reducing such conflict and increasing the positive affect in the husband-wife relationship may have considerable effects on the phenomenon of running away.

Burke   and   Burkhead[161] recalled that the early psychological literature attributed runaway behavior to a specific mental disorder in children. Early follow-up data suggested that running away was related to future maladaptive behavior. Researchers in the 1960s who rejected this perspective viewed running away as merely a function of normal child development and suggested that youth run away in search of adventure and independence. More recently, researchers have attributed running away to a variety of family dynamics and learned problem solving methods. From all 3 perspectives, however, the literature has primarily attempted to describe runaway children rather than to analyze the function of the behavior (p. 79).

Burke and Burkhead[162] suggested that future research must attempt to do more than provide descriptions of runaway children. Several investigators, according to Burke and Burkhead, have suggested that researchers will learn more by analyzing the differences between runaways and nonrunaways in terms of personality and psychological characteristics and family and social relations.

> Separate analysis of these aspects of runaway children
> may begin to shed some light on the etiology of this
> behavior. In addition, it appears that methods of coping
> with stress and solving problems are directly related to

running away. Research which identifies problem solving strategies employed by runaways and nonrunaways and offers alternatives to potential maladaptive problem-solving should prove beneficial in the treatment of runaway children. Examination of variables related to the family life experiences of runaways and nonrunaways may also provide more information regarding the family variables that relate to runaway behavior. Analysis of parental modeling, methods by which parents cope with stress and solve problems and methods of discipline used by parents appear to be needed. This information may lead to the development of family intervention methods to treat the runaway child (p. 79).

Roberts[163] suggested that his typology for runaways, based upon a 5-point continuum of parent-youth conflict, be tested for applicability to other populations of runaway youth. He believed that with further research, clinicians will have better clues and intervention guides to determine whether treatment for runaways in one category should be different from treatment for those in another category. He believed that assessment scales and diagnostic indicators:

> will be incomplete if they do not include assessment of the individual in the context of his or her interactional systems, such as the family. Fundamental to comprehensive assessment is an analysis of how well each adolescent relates to the significant systems in his or her life (p. 395).

Edelbrock[164] cited a shortcoming of current research when he said that we have learned little by comparing runaways with nonrunaways who have not come to the attention of human service professionals. He suggested that we gain more insight into factors contributing to runaway behavior by identifying the characteristics of runaway youth among a sample of troubled youth. From a subject pool of 2,967 children who had been referred for mental health services and 1,300 who had not, Edelbrock (1980) tried to determine the incidence of running away in the 2 groups, and characteristics of disturbed youth who ran away, the behavior problems associated with running away, and possible differences between disturbed and nondisturbed runaways. He found that stealing, lying, truancy, and substance abuse, behaviors which were correlated with delinquency, were also correlated with running away. He also found the incidence of running away to be much greater in the disturbed group, and suggested that this may indicate that more serious emotional problems were related to runaway behavior.

Burke and Burkhead[165] believed that the usefulness of future research would be enhanced if the number of times a youth has run away is explicitly taken into account. Separating youths who run away only once from those who run many times appeared to them to have contributed to the understanding of running away. Studies that focus on the 2 groups separately may provide more relevant information regarding each kind of runaway behavior (p. 74).

NOTES

[1] D. Walker, *Runaway Youth: Annotated Bibliography and Literature Overview* (Washington, D.C.: Office of Social Services and Human Development, Department of Health and Human Services, 1975).

[2] *To Whom Do They Belong?: A Profile of America's Runaway Youth and the Programs that Help Them* (Washington, D.C.: The National Network of Runaway and Youth Services, Inc., 1985).

[3] K. Libertoff, "The Runaway Child in America: A Social History," *Journal of Family Issues* 22 (June 1980): 151-164.

[4] W. Burke and E. Burkhead, "Runaway Children in America: A Review of the Literature," *Education and Treatment of Children* 12 (February 1989): 73-81; H. Fishman, *Treating Troubled Adolescents* (New York: Basic Books, 1988).

[5] B. Justice and D. Duncan, "Running Away: An Epidemic Problem of Adolescence," *Adolescence* 11 (Fall 1976): 365-371.

[6] This and all subsequent references to The National Network of Runaway and Youth Services are from the work cited in note 2 above and may be simply referred to as "National Network" or "National Network report."

[7] This and all subsequent references to D. Walker are from the work cited in note 1 above.

[8] "Runaways: Rising U.S. Worry," *U.S. News and World Report* (September 3, 1973), p. 34.

[9] D. Rader, "I Want To Die So I Won't Hurt No More," *Parade* (August 2-7, 1985).

[10] R. Johnson and M. Carter, "Flight of the Young: Why Children Run Away From Their Homes," *Adolescence* 15 (Summer 1980): 483-489.

[11] T. Gulotta, "Leaving Home: Family Relationships of the Runaway Child," *Social Casework: The Journal of Contemporary Social Work* (February 1979): 111-114.

[12] See note 11 above.

[13] *U.S. News and World Report* (May 2, 1975), p. 49.

[14] See note 4 above.

[15] T. Brennan, "Mapping the Diversity among Runaways: A Descriptive Multivariate Analysis of Selected Social Psychological Background Conditions," *Journal of Family Issues* 1 (June 1980): 189-209; T. Brennan, D. Huizinga and D. Elliott, *The Social Psychology of Runaways* (Lexington, MA: D.C. Heath and Co., 1978); L. Olson, E. Liebow, F. Mannino and M. Shore, "Runaway Children Twelve Years Later: A Follow-up," *Journal of Family Issues* 1 (June 1980): 165-188; A. Roberts, "Adolescent Runaways in Suburbia: A New Typology," *Adolescence* 17 (Summer 1982): 387-396; D. Walker; R. Young, W. Godfrey, B. Matthews and G. Adams, "Runaways: A Review of Negative Consequences," *Family Relations* 32 (1983): 275-281.

[16] T. Brennan, D. Huizinga and D. Elliott (see note 15 above).

[17] E. Hughes, "Running Away: A 50-50 Chance to Survive?" *USA Today Magazine* 118 (September 1989): 64-66.

[18] See note 11 above; A. Roberts, "Stress and Coping Patterns Among Adolescent Runaways," *Journal of Social Service Research* 5 (1982): 15-27; R. Young, W. Godfrey, B. Matthews and G. Adams (see note 15 above).

[19] T. Brennan, D. Huizinga and D. Elliott (see note 15 above); See note 11 above; A. Roberts (see note 18 above).

[20] See note 11 above; A. Roberts (see note 18 above); R. Young, W. Godfrey, B. Matthews and G. Adams (see note 15 above).

[21] A. Roberts (see note 18 above).

[22] J. Palenski and H. Launer, "The 'Process' of Running Away: A Redefinition," *Adolescence* 22 (Summer 1987): 347-362.

[23] P. Kammer and D. Schmidt, "Counseling Runaway Adolescents," *The School Counselor* 35 (American School Counselor Association, November 1987).

[24] P. Rich, "The Juvenile Justice System and Its Treatment of the Juvenile: An Overview,"*Adolescence* 17 (Spring 1982): 141-152.

[25] National Network (see notes 2 and 6 above).

[26] F. Dunford and T. Brennan, "A Taxonomy of Runaway Youth,"*Social Service Review* (September 1976): 457-470.

[27] F. Nye, *Runaways: A Report for Parents* (Pullman, WA: Extension Bulletin 1743. Cooperative Extension, Washington State University, 1980): 1-10.

[28] See note 9 above.

[29] L. Morgan, "Desperate Odds," *Seventeen* (March 1989): 257.

[30] See note 17 above.

[31] See note 29 above.

[32] Opinion Research Corporation, *National Statistical Survey On Runaway Youth.* Report prepared for the Office of Youth Development and Office of Human Development, Department of Health, Education, and Welfare (1976).

[33] See note17 above.

[34] See note 23 above.

[35] See note 17 above.

[36] in C. Berman, "The Runaway Crisis," *McCall"s* 15 (January 1988) 113-116.

[37] See note 23 above.

[38] P. Hersch, "Coming of Age On City Streets," *Psychology Today* 22 (January 1988): 28-32.

[39] T. Gulotta, "Runaway: Reality or Myth," *Adolescence* 13 (Winter 1978): 543-549.

[40] See note 9 above.

41 See note 38 above.

42 See note 38 above.

43 See note 38 above.

44 See note 9 above.

45 T. Brennan, D. Huizinga and D. Elliott (see note 15 above); R. Jenkins, "The Runaway Reaction," *American Journal of Psychiatry* 128 (1971): 60-65; R. Shellow, J. Schamp, E. Liebow and E. Unger, "Suburban Runaways of the 1960's," *Monograph of the Society for Research in Child Development* 32 3, Serial No. 111 (1967): 1-50.

46 N. Speck, D. Ginther and J. Helton, "Runaways: Who Will Run Away Again? *Adolescence* 23 (Winter 1988): 881-888.

47 See note 46 above.

48 See note 46 above.

49 M. Janus, A. Burgess and A. McCormack, "Histories of Sexual Abuse in Adolescent Male Runaways," *Adolescence* 22 (Summer 1987): 405-417.

50 F. Nye and C. Edelbrock, "Introduction–Some Social Characteristics of Runaways," *Journal of Family Issues* 1 (June 1980): 147-150.

51 See note 9 above.

52 See note 50 above.

53 G. Adams, T. Gulotta and M. Clancy, "Homeless Adolescents: A Descriptive Study of Similarities and Differences Between Runaways and Throwaways,"*Adolescence* 20 (Fall 1985): 715-724.

54 L. Blood and R. D'Angelo, "A Progress Research Report On Value Issues In Conflict Between Runaways and Their Parents," *Journal of Marriage and the Family* (August 1974): 486-491; C. English, "Leaving Home: A Typology of Runaways," *Society* 10 (July/August 1973): 22-25; D. Gottlieb and J. Chafetz, "Dynamics of Familial, Generational Conflict and Reconciliation," *Youth and Society* 9 (December 1977): 213-224; Opinion Research Corporation (see note 32 above); S. Wolk and J. Brandon, "Runaway Adolescents' Perseptions of Parents and Self," *Adolescence* XII (Summer 1977): 175-187.

[55] G. Adams and G. Munro, "Portrait of the North American Runaway: A Critical Review," *Journal of Youth and Adolescence* 8 (1979): 359-373.

[56] P. Post and D. McCoard, "Needs and Self-Concept of Runaway Adolescents," *School Counselor* 41 (January 1994): 212-219.

[57] E. Spillane-Grieco, "Characteristics of a Helpful Relationship: A Study of Empathic Understanding and Positive Regard Between Runaways and Their Parents," *Adolescence* XIX (1984): 63-75.

[58] E. Spillane-Grieco, "Feelings and Perceptions of Parents of Runaways," *Child Welfare* LXIII (March/April 1984): 159-166.

[59] T. Brennan, D. Huizinga and D. Elliott (see note 15 above).

[60] See note 53 above.

[61] See note 50 above.

[62] J. Goldmeier and R. Dean, "The Runaway: Person, Problem, or Situation?," *Crime and Delinquency* (October 1973): 539-544.

[63] L. Olson, E. Liebow, F. Mannino and M. Shore (see note 15 above).

[64] S. Englander, "Some Self-Reported Correlates of Runaway Behavior in Adolescent Females," *Journal of Consulting and Clinical Psychology* 52 (1984): 484-485.

[65] See note 23 above.

[66] T. Brennan (see note 15 above); T. Brennan, D. Huizinga and D. Elliott (see note 15 above); W. Burke and E. Burkhead (see note 4 above); See note 26 above; S. Gutierres and F. Reich, "A Developmental Perspective On Runaway Behavior: Its Relationship to Child Abuse," *Child Welfare* LX (February 1981): 89-94; See note 3 above.

[67] p. 75. See note 4 above.

[68] L. Blood and R. D'Angelo (see note 54 above); T. Brennan, D. Huizinga and D. Elliott (see note 15 above); See note 3 above; See note 18 above.

[69] L. Blood and R. D'Angelo (see note 54 above) cited in W. Burke and E. Burkhead (see note 4 above).

[70] W. Burke and E. Burkhead (see note 4 above).

[71] W. Burke and E. Burkhead (see note 4 above).

[72] T. Brennan, D. Huizinga and D. Elliott (see note 15 above); R. Jenkins, "Classification of Behavior Problems of Children," *American Journal of Psychiatry* 125 (February 1969): 68-75; R. Shellow, J. Schamp, E. Liebow and E. Unger (see note 45 above); H. Stierlin, "A Family Perspective On Adolescent Runaways," *Archives of General Psychiatry* 29 (July 1973): 56-62.

[73] S. Jorgensen, H. Thornberg and J. Williams, "The Experience of Running Away: Perceptions of Adolescents Seeking Help in a Shelter Care Facility," *High School Journal* (December 1980): 87-96.

[74] R. Jenkins (see note 72 above).

[75] F. Nye, "A Theoretical Perspective on Running Away," *Journal of Family Issues* 1 (June 1980): 274-299.

[76] W. Burke and E. Burkhead (see note 4 above).

[77] S. Gutierres and F. Reich (see note 66 above).

[78] S. Gutierres and F. Reich (see note 66 above).

[79] W. Burke and E. Burkhead (see note 4 above).

[80] L. Ambrosino, *Runaways* (Boston: Beacon, 1971).

[81] R. Shellow, J. Schamp, E. Liebow and E. Unger (see note 45 above).

[82] L. Homer, "Community Based Resources for Runaway Girls," *Social Casework* 54 (1973): 473-479.

[83] See note 46 above.

[84] See note 82 above.

[85] S. Sharlin and M. Mor-Barak, "Runaway Girls in Distress: Motivation, Background, and Personality," *Adolescence* 27 (Summer 1992): 387-406.

[86] W. Burke and E. Burkhead (see note 4 above).

[87] See note 73 above.

[88] See note 22 above.

[89] C. Brothers, "The Gestalt Theory of Healthy Aggression in Beyond-Control Youth," *Psychotherapy* 23 (Winter 1986): 578-585.

[90] See note 5 above; J. Orten and S. Soll, "Runaway Children and Their Families: A Treatment Typology," *Journal of Family Issues* 1 (June, 1980): 249-261. K. Ostensen, "The Runaway

Crisis: Is Family Therapy the Answer?," *American Journal of Family Therapy* 9 (Fall, 1981); H. Stierlin (see note 72 above).

[91] H. Stierlin (see note 72 above).

[92] See note 10 above.

[93] T. Brennan (see note 15 above); T. Brennan, D. Huizinga and D. Elliott (see note 15 above); M. Howell, E. Emmong and D. Frank, "Reminiscences of Runaway Adolescents," *American Journal of Orthopsychiatry* 43 (October 1973): 840-853; R. Shellow, J. Schamp, E. Liebow and E. Unger (see note 45 above).

[94] L. Olson, E. Liebow, F. Mannino and M. Shore (see note 15 above.

[95] S. Gutierres and F. Reich (see note 66 above).

[96] "Why Children Are Running Away in Record Numbers," *U.S. News and World Report* (January 17, 1977): 62.

[97] P. Kurtz, G. Kurtz and J. Jarvis, "Problems of Maltreated Runaway Youth," *Adolescence* 26 (Fall 1991): 543-555.

[98] See note 13 above.

[99] H. Fishman, *Treating Troubled Adolescents* (New York: Basic Books, 1988).

[100] See note 38 above.

[101] T. Brennan, D. Huizinga and D. Elliott (see note 15 above).

[102] T. Brennan, D. Huizinga and D. Elliott (see note 15 above).

[103] T. Brennan, D. Huizinga and D. Elliott (see note 15 above).

[104] A. Roberts (see note 18 above).

[105] A. Roberts (see note 18 above).

[106] S. Fors and D. Rojek, "A Comparison of Drug Involvement Between Runaways and School Youths," *Journal of Drug Education* 21 (1991): 13-25.

[107] A. Roberts (see note 18 above).

[108] R. Jessor and S. Jessor, *Problem Behavior and Psychological Development: A Longitudinal Stude of Youth* (New York: Academic Press, 1977).

[109] See note 75 above.

[110] See note 75 above.

[111] See note 75 above.

[112] See note 75 above.

[113] See note 75 above.

[114] See note 75 above.

[115] See note 17 above.

[116] See note 17 above.

[117] See note 36 above.

[118] See note 36 above.

[119] see note 23 above.

[120] J. Comer, "Kids On the Run," *Parents* (January 1988): 146.

[121] T. Brennan, D. Huizinga and D. Elliott (see note 15 above).

[122] L. Blood and R. D'Angelo (see note 54 above).

[123] D. Gottlieb and J. Chafetz (see note 54 above).

[124] T. Brennan, D. Huizinga and D. Elliott (see note 15 above).

[125] A. Roberts (see note 15 above).

[126] A. Roberts (see note 15 above).

[127] C. English (see note 54 above).

[128] H. Stierlin (see note 72 above).

[129] H. Stierlin (see note 72 above).

[130] See note 26 above.

[131] T. Brennan, D. Huiainga and D. Elliott (see note 15 above).

[132] See note 75 above.

[133] A Roberts, *Runaways and Nonrunaways in an American Suburb* (New York: The John Jay Press, 1981); A. Roberts (see note 15 above).

[134] See note 17 above.

[135] See note 120 above.

[136] See note 38 above.

[137] See note 38 above.

[138] See note 49 above.

[139] See note 49 above.

[140] L. Olson, E. Liebow, F. Mannino and M. Shore (see note 15 above).

[141] F. Nye, *Runaways: Some Critical Issues For Professionals and Society* (Pullman, WA: Extension Bulletin 0744. Cooperative Extension, Washington State University, 1981): 1-11.

[142] See note 23 above.

[143] See note 23 above.

[144] See note 23 above.

[145] See note 62 above.

[146] See note 75 above.

[147] See note 23 above.

[148] See note 23 above.

[149] See note 89 above.

[150] R. Loeb, T. Burke and C. Boglarsky, "A Large-Scale Comparison of Perspectives On Parenting Between Teenage Runaways and Nonrunaways," *Adolescence* 21 (Winter 1986): 921-930.

[151] S. Wolk and J. Brandon (see note 54 above).

[152] S. Wolk and J. Brandon (see note 54 above).

[153] See note 53 above.

[154] See note 133 above.

[155] See note 58 above.

[156] H. Stierlin, *Separating Parents and Adolescents* (New York: Jason Aronson, Inc., 1981); H. Stierlin (see note 72 above).

[157] H. Stierlin, *Separating Parents* (see note 156 above), p. 61.

[158] See note 75 above.

[159] See note 75 above.

[160] See note 75 above.

[161] W. Burke and E. Burkhead (see note 4 above).

[162] W. Burke and E. Burkhead (see note 4 above).

[163] A. Roberts (see note 15 above).

[164] C. Edelbrock, "Running Away From Home: Incidence and Correlates Among Children and Youth Referred For Mental Health Services," *Journal of Family Issues* 1 (June 1980): 210-229.

[165] See note 5 above.

III

Family Systems Theory and Runaways

Family Systems Theory, derived from general systems theory, addresses individual phenomena from a contextual perspective and appears to offer a broad conceptual and integrative framework to the study and understanding of the runaway phenomenon which is lacking in the literature to date. This theory emphasizes the mutually reciprocal influence of adolescents, parents, families, school, and other systems. The systems perspective "has demonstrated its efficacy in the physical, biological, and social sciences; its application to the study of human beings has been equally fruitful".[1]

A review of the literature has demonstrated that much of the thinking, research, and treatment with regard to the runaway phenomenon has come from the perspective of individual psychology. The philosophical assumptions of individual psychology are firmly based upon the logical positivist-empirical tradition of Western science. This tradition has evolved and developed from the mechanistic world view of Newton in which the material world is described as like a machine consisting of elementary parts or basic building blocks. From this Western scientific, individual perspective reality is considered external, and the world is understood to be deterministic. Scientific "laws" are in operation, the understanding of which reveals some absolute truths about reality. Becvar and Becvar[2] explain that, within this tradition, the world is understood as consisting of subjects and objects in which one event causes a reaction from or an effect upon another. One event is held responsible for another, or one event is blamed for another. Solutions to problems are attempted by seeking an answer to the question "Why?" (p. 4).

From these traditional beliefs of the physical sciences the behavioral sciences developed theories "that described human behavior as determined either by internal events or external environmental sequences in relation to which we may react" (p. 4).[3] Accepting the values and basic assumptions of this Western scientific tradition, behavioral scientists believed that their attention should focus on root causes, previous events which led to later problems, and specific individual behaviors in order to find solutions.

The theories of psychology developed by Freud, Skinner, Jung and others focus on the individual and are based upon similar fundamental beliefs.

Becvar and Becvar[4] claim that an examination of a variety of individual psychologies, intrapsychic theories, learning theories, and therapies reveal that each is based on a foundation that includes most of the following:

> Asks Why?
> Linear cause/effect
> Subject/object dualism
> Either/or dichotomies
> Value-free science
> Deterministic/reactive
> Laws and lawlike external reality
> Historical focus
> Individualistic
> Reductionistic
> Absolutistic (pp. 5-6)

Systems theory is based upon a very different set of assumptions. The systems perspective takes a broad ecological view which looks at the world in terms of the constant, yet ever-changing aspects of it and of ourselves. This view is consistent with that of Eastern religion and philosophy in which all phenomena are viewed as interrelated and interdependent. Within this framework an integrated whole, whose properties cannot be reduced to those of its parts, is called a system.[5] Assumptions of systems theory, however, are not necessarily contrasted to those of the individual perspective in an either-or dichotomy. A systemic perspective, instead, integrates the traditional world view and individual psychology with an interactive, contextual view.

The idea that all of nature is intricately related and embedded in a larger whole has also been expressed more recently in the area of relativity physics (p. 579).[6] Capra[7] discusses the challenges that physicists faced when they attempted to understand atomic phenomena. The observations and insights from quantum physics bring into question the concept of matter as separate from mind and of the idea that matter can be reduced to basic building blocks. The conceptual revolutions which have occurred in the field of physics in this century, led by the work of Albert Einstein, have revealed, says Capra, "the limitations of the mechanistic world view and lead to an organic, ecological view of the world which shows great similarities to the views of mystics of all ages and traditions" (p. 47). The atomic experiments in the early 1900s demonstrated that conventional concepts alone were not adequate to describe a new reality in which, for example, subatomic units of matter appear sometimes as particles and other times as waves. This reality is in sharp contrast to the Newtonian, mechanistic view of the universe in which the world is believed to consist of "separate objects which can be broken down into basic building blocks which interact mechanically in specific, definite cause and effect relationships" (p. 578).[8]

> The new world view emerging from modern physics can be characterized by words like organic, holistic, and ecological. It might also be called a systems view . . . The universe is no longer seen as a machine, made up of a multitude of objects, but has to be pictured as one indivisible, dynamic whole whose parts are essentially interrelated and can be understood only as patterns of a cosmic process (p. 77-78).[9]

Modern physicists now view the universe as "an indivisible whole comprised of dynamic relationships that include observers, as well as their minds, in that which is observed".[10] Briggs and Peat[11] refer to this as a "looking glass universe" in which the observer and the observed mutually influence each other. The very act of studying changes that which is being studied.

The systems vision of reality, says Capra,[12] "is based on awareness of the essential interrelatedness and interdependence of all phenomena–physical, biological, psychological, social, and cultural (p. 265). This approach emphasizes basic principles of organization instead of concentrating on basic building blocks or basic substances. Says Capra:

> Every organism–from the smallest bacterium through the wide range of plants and animals to humans–is an integrated whole and thus a living system. . . . The same

aspects of wholeness are exhibited by social systems–
such as an ant hill, a beehive, or a human family–and by
eco-systems that consist of a variety of organisms and
inanimate matter in mutual interaction. The activity of
systems involves the simultaneous and mutually
interdependent interaction between multiple components
(p. 266).

Assuming that the observations in the world of the "new
physics" are accurate and that they may be applicable to the field of
psychology, "the implications for the mental health profession are
profound . . . we don't just study people, we influence who they are and
what they might become and vice versa" (pp. 335-6).[13] Both the new
physics and systems theory pose challenges to the fundamental
assumptions of the logical positivist-empirical scientific tradition.
Among these challenges, according to Becvar and Becvar, are:

1) A reality may exist independent of us, but we cannot
know that reality.

2) The reality that exists for us and the reality we can
observe is relative to the theory we use as a metaphor for
that reality.

3) What we can observe is a function of the means
(instruments, tools, and machines) we use to measure the
phenomena of interest (phenomena that exist and are
meaningful) and of our theories which suggest what
might be "out there."

4) Reality is a dynamic, evolving, changing entity.

5) To observe a phenomenon is to change the nature of
the phenomenon observed.

6) Phenomena observed take on characteristics of the
theory or model used to guide and systematize the
observations.

7) The appropriate unit of analysis is not elementary
parts but relationships, which should be the basis of all
definitions (p. 336 .).

Systems theory moves our focus toward relationships between and among systems and subsystems and away from individual issues in isolation. This is not to say that individual issues are non-existent or unimportant. Individual issues, from the systems perspective, are viewed in relational and contextual terms. Instead of subject acting upon object in a linear cause-and-effect manner, "we are all concurrently subjects and objects; we are all involved in each other's destiny. Reality is not external to us but is created by us as we bring our own personal perceptions to bear on it and give meaning and order to it (p. 11).[14] Emphasis is placed on mutual influence, reciprocity, and shared responsibility.

When seeking solutions to troubling issues, we do not ask why something happened, according to Becvar and Becvar.[15] We rather ask what is going on in an effort to discover patterns. From this wholistic perspective, the meaning of events is derived from a focus on process and context rather than on the events themselves or the individuals in isolation. Focus is on the present. We "examine here-and-now interactions rather than look to history for antecedent causes" (p. 9).

Family systems theory, or systems theory as it applies to the study of individuals and families, is, according to Becvar and Becvar,[16] based on a foundation which includes the following:

Asks What?
Reciprocal causality
Wholistic
Dialectical
Subjective/perceptual
Freedom of choice/proactive
Patterns
Here-and-now focus
Relational
Contextual
Relativistic (p. 8)

Normal families function according to some key principles or concepts that apply to all systems. These concepts have emerged in the various models of systems family therapy and are fundamental to the conceptualization of the family from the systems perspective.

The concept of circular causality defines a family system as a group of individuals interrelated so that a change in any one member affects other individuals and the family group as a whole. The changes in other individuals and in the group in turn affect the first individual in a circular chain of influence. Causality is viewed as circular rather than linear.

Family systems theory conceptualizes the family as "an open system that functions in relation to its broader sociocultural context and that evolves over the life cycle" (p. 9).[17] The systems concepts of openness and closedness applied to families refer to "the boundaries a family establishes among family members and between itself and other systems" (p. 17).[18] The boundaries of a family system are defined by the patterns of behavior/communication which allow a family to establish its distinct identity. The degree of rigidity of the boundaries of a system serves to regulate the amount of information which can enter from outside the system. The more open the family system, the more information/energy exchange the members allow from each other or the family allows from other systems. The more closed a family system, the less information exchange takes place. As with stability and change, a functional family system will maintain a healthy balance between the two extremes.

Patterns of enmeshment or disengagement may be observed in some dysfunctional families. Enmeshment, a pattern of extreme closeness and intensity in family interactions, often creates poorly differentiated boundaries among family members. Disengagement can be observed when there seems to be a relative absence of strong connections within the family and relationship ties between family members are weak. A pattern of rigidity may also be encountered in families and is demonstrated as an inability of the family to change from the status quo when circumstances would seem to indicate that change is appropriate. Fishman[19] sees overprotectiveness as still another pattern which may be seen in some dysfunctional families. Here is an inappropriately high degree of concern on the part of a parent or parents toward the children which often inhibits the children from developing autonomy and competence.

The concept of nonsummativity views the family as a whole which is greater that the sum of its parts. The interactional patterns and family organization involve an "interlocking of the behavior of its members" (p. 9).[20] It is necessary to attend to the "pattern that connects".[21]

According to the principle of equifinality, the same outcome may result from different origins, and the same origin may lead to different outcomes. Bertalanffy[22] says that equifinality is "the tendency towards a characteristic final state from different initial states and in different ways based upon dynamic interaction in an open system attaining a steady state" (p. 46). One family, for example, may become dysfunctional in response to a crisis while another family rallies in response to the same crisis. The concept of equifinality, according to Becvar and Becvar,[23] precludes the need for an historical perspective. With systems:

> The important question for the therapist becomes "what" rather than "why," The focus is on the here and now. . . The key is the pattern. . . . in many cases, it is the attempted solutions, or the repetition of dysfunctional patterns which maintain a so-called "problem," which are in fact problematic (p. 15).

From the family systems perspective all behavior is regarded as communication. Just as it is impossible not to behave, it is impossible not to communicate. Verbal communication is used to transmit information and is often called the "content" or "report" aspect. Non-verbal communication, the "relationship" or "command" aspect, conveys how the information is to be taken and defines the nature of the relationship. Patterns of behavior/communication which may be observed in dysfunctional families include complementary and symmetrical behavior sequences which can escalate to a schism, or separation.[24] The complementary pattern can be observed as a series of reciprocal behaviors such as with a husband who is angry and a wife who complains of headaches. The pattern escalates as the husband becomes angrier and the wife complains of more frequent and severe headaches. A symmetrical pattern can be seen when the individuals exhibit more and more of the same behaviors. In a heated argument, for example, each person becomes more and more agitated and unwilling to back down and violence may erupt.

Both explicit and implicit relationship rules function to organize family interaction and to maintain a stable system by prescribing and limiting members' behavior. Family rules provide expectations about roles, actions, and consequences. Through the operation of the "redundancy principle," a family tends to interact in repetitious sequences, so that the family operations are governed by a relatively small set of patterned and predictable rules (p. 10).[25]

Homeostasis, morphostasis, and morphogenesis are related concepts which are important to family systems theory. Homeostasis refers to a system's tendency to seek and capacity to maintain stability and equilibrium (p. 31).[26] The two related concepts of morphegenesis and morphostasis are described by Speer.[27] Morphostasis is similar to homeostasis, while morphogenesis refers to behavior within a system which allows for growth and change. An appropriate balance of both change (morphogenesis) and stability (morphostasis) is necessary to the functioning of healthy family systems as well as other kinds of systems. "All family members contribute to the homeostatic balance through a mutually reinforcing feedback loop, such as in complementary or reciprocal behavior" (p. 10).[28]

A number of models of normal family functioning and family therapy are grounded in a systems orientation. Considerable overlap exists among these and other systems models, and they are "remarkably free in general from any major contradiction or inconsistency" (p. 25).[29] Where differences do appear, they reflect a more selective emphasis on a particular aspect of family functioning rather than substantive differences. A brief description of several of these models will demonstrate the variety of approaches which exist within the systems framework.

The structural model, developed by Minuchin and his colleagues,[30] emphasizes the importance of family organization for the functioning of the family unit as a whole and the well-being of its members. Problems are common to all normal families, according to Minuchin,[31] and ". . . they are constantly struggling with these problems and negotiating the compromises that make a life in common possible" (p. 16). Minuchin emphasizes the importance of hierarchy in the effectively functioning family system. The clear definition of family boundaries, including parental, spouse, and child subsystem boundaries, is necessary to healthy family functioning according to this model. All family patterns are viewed as points on a continuum with enmeshment at one extreme and disengagement at the other. Relationship patterns which fall at either extreme on the continuum impede healthy communication. The boundaries of the system must be clear and firm but flexible enough to promote both autonomy and interdependence. Minuchin[32] urges therapists to view the family as "a social system in transformation. . . . With this orientation, many more families who enter therapy would be seen and treated as average families in transitional situations, suffering the pains of accommodation to new circumstances" (p. 60).

The strategic model of family therapy is represented by the Palo Alto group of Watzlawick, Weakland and Fisch, the Milan group of Selvini Palazzoli, Boscolo, Cecchin and Prata, and the problem-solving approach of Haley.[33] Strategic therapists in the Palo Alto group are concerned primarily with how families attempt to resolve normal difficulties in day to day living. They focus on how families maintain a problem by the ways in which they attempt to solve it. The pattern of the attempted solution becoming the problem is the pattern which requires therapeutic change.

The Palo Alto group and the Milan group view normal families as extremely flexible. Dysfunctional families often demonstrate rigidity and a lack of alternatives in response to developmental and environmental changes. According to Hoffman,[34] "The positive connotation, or 'reframe', is a therapeutic device that may be one of the Milan group's most original inventions" (p. 289). Using a positive connotation, or "reframe", the therapist avoids a stance of linear causality which would define the behavior as serving a positive function of bringing the parents together. The therapist instead would define or reframe all the symptomatic behaviors of the family members as serving to preserve the cohesion of the family group.[35]

What some researchers may report as "reasons" or "causes" for running away could be "reframed" as context descriptions. For example, Brennan, Huizinga and Elliott[36] and Wolk and Brandon[37] say that females appear to run "because of" a restrictive environment, and males appear to run "due to" a detached or rejecting family. Gulotta[38] says that incestual or abuse problems are major "causes" of leaving home. Adams and Munro[39] suspect that some adolescents run "because of" their growing disillusionment with existing societal values. Young, Godfrey, Matthews and Adams[40] say, "Perhaps extreme parental expectations, or family interaction dysfunctions are the 'causal' pressures that push adolescents into coping by running" (p. 277). From the systems perspective, attempts to establish a linear cause and effect sequence make no sense. Instead, the relationships

between and among the described contexts and an adolescent's
running away are viewed as mutually influencing in a pattern of
circular causality.

Haley[41] developed a strategic problem-solving approach to
family therapy which selectively focuses on certain family variables
involving power and organization within the family that he believes
are relevant to therapeutic change. Symptoms arise when families
are unable to adjust to life cycle transitions and become "stuck"
within a phase. For example, the problem "mad young people" have
in leaving home—which may be expressed in schizophrenic
symptoms, substance abuse, or other behavior disorders—is seen as
a family separation problem related to the crisis of transition to the
next life phase.[42] In order to successfully move to the next
developmental phase, a family must have clear subsystem
boundaries where parents establish clear rules and provide both
nurture and discipline for their children.

The importance of working with the family of origin and the
concept of "differentiation" are central to the approach of Bowen. A
major contribution to family theory is Bowen's thinking about the
roles played by triangles in family interaction. "Triangulation is a
process that occurs in all families, all social groups, as twosomes
form to the exclusion of, or against, a third" (p. 29).[43] For Bowen, a
two-person system will, under stress, form a three-person system.
When tensions arise between two persons, for example, one might
attempt to relieve the tension by "triangling in" (p. 29).[44] Bowen
sees networks of triangles as strongly linked and reactive to one
another. The triangle is also an essential part of Haley's theory of
pathological systems and of Minuchin's structural approach.

Bowen's concept of "differentiation" is important in his
view of the family system. He noticed that dysfunctional families
often exhibited a clinging interdependence or "stuck togetherness"
which he called the "undifferentiated family ego mass" (p. 31).[45]
The lack of differentiation, which is similar to Minuchin's notion of
enmeshment, was, for Bowen, a sign of trouble in a family. These
concepts suggest that when individual members of a family achieve
and maintain a high degree of differentiation, the family and its
members will do well.

Both Satir and Whitaker pursue an experiential approach to
family therapy that is highly intuitive and relatively atheoretical (p.
23).[46] Satir integrates communications and humanistic
orientations.[47] For Satir healthy families include members whose

sense of self-worth is high. Communication is clear, direct, and honest. Rules for family members are flexible, appropriate, and open to negotiation. And the healthy family has open and hopeful links to larger societal systems.

For Whitaker the sense of the family as an integrated whole, with the separation of parent and child generations along with flexibility of rules and roles, is fundamental.[48] A healthy family is an open system which relates to the extended family and society while maintaining the primacy of the nuclear family unit. There is a healthy balance between intimacy and separateness and between dependency and autonomy. The dimension of time is central with emphasis on the process of becoming. " . . . less attention is given to the past and more to current, shared affective experience and to the totality of the family as an interactive, self-maintaining system."[49]

The key concepts of systems theory and family therapy can be linked to the understanding of the phenomenon of adolescent runaways. Watzlawick, Weakland and Fisch[50] discuss a hypothetical example of an adolescent who begins to stay out all night or run away for longer periods of time. The child may be attempting to gain more independence and "differentiation" from the family by pushing the limits or boundaries of allowable behavior. From the adolescent's point of view, the family system may need to be more open to allow for a wider range of behaviors. Parents may react by continuing to hold to the limits in what Watzlawick, Weakland and Fisch call a "game without end".[51] In this situation a complementary sequence of behavior/communication develops as a struggle of more of one behavior (limit setting) with more of another behavior (running away). Here the symptomatic cycle of problem-becoming-solution-becoming-problem is played out.

In a family in which an adolescent runs away, the runaway behavior may be followed by the illness of a parent, or by increased focus on the child. This may then be followed by the child's return and increased attention toward the parent or by further behaviors of distancing or differentiating from the family. Whatever the behavior/communication, and whatever the sequence, the systems concept of circular causality sees each individual as affecting the other individuals and the total family system. One event does not "cause" another, but each event in turn affects the other events, individuals, and the family system as a whole in a circular pattern of influence.

The concept of equifinality may also be demonstrated in the families of adolescent runaways. One family may respond to a runaway event by reorganizing and developing more appropriate family rules which reflect the adolescent's communicating a need for more independence and differentiation. Another family may respond by attempting to enforce the family "rules" and hold the family boundaries unchanged. Still another family may develop more rigid boundaries and move toward a more closed system in which enmeshment is evident. These examples of family patterns also illustrate the concept of nonsummativity and the role of family rules as each family demonstrates its own unique organization and pattern of interaction.

An adolescent's running away may function to maintain homeostasis, or balance, in the family system. Perhaps stress in the parental subsystem or in a sibling subsystem is threatening the stability of the family. A runaway event may serve to redirect the stress in the family and maintain its viability as a system. Likewise, an adolescent runaway event may push the family system toward morphogenesis which allows for growth and change.

Watzlawick, Weakland and Fisch[52] see cycles of behavior in which "problem becomes solution becomes problem" as examples of first order change being attempted when second order change may be necessary. First order change may be described as minor fluctuations within existing limits of behavior. Second order changes apply to any situations in which "the usual range of behaviors is no longer applicable because of developments in the outer field or inside the system itself" (p. 198).[53] Second order change applies to a change in the rules and/or to a change in the rules about changing the rules.

Watzlawick, Weakland and Fisch[54] use a metaphor for these two kinds of change by noting the difference between pressing the gas pedal and changing gears when driving a car (p. 9). Within a family second order change may be a part of the natural developmental process over time and may be set off by any major shift in the rules governing one or more relationships in the family. If the issue around the symptomatic behavior(s), whether it be an adolescent running away or some other behaviors, involves the range of allowable behaviors in the family, second order change needs to be negotiated, according to Watzlawick, Weakland and Fisch.[55] The therapist's task becomes that of reorganizing these destructive cycles and intervening to disrupt the cycle and facilitate second order change.

According to Becvar and Becvar:[56]

> Adolescents, reflecting the ever increasing input from other systems, may want more rapid change in the family system than that desired by their parents. Thus the parents of adolescents often act to modify or restrict the nature of the rate of change. . . . if the system is to be functional, change needs to be accommodated by the system in some way, to some degree. The contract between parent and child that was effective when the child was younger will not be functional for the adolescent-parent relationship (p. 17).

Becvar and Becvar[57] use a systems model to describe the functioning of a healthy family system. They suggest the following propositions:

> 1) A system needs to be stable and yet able to change or to be flexible.
>
> 2) Families like individuals go through developmental stages.
>
> 3) The family needs to be both open and closed.
>
> 4) Family members need to be individuals and yet feel like they belong.
>
> 5) Communication is feedback and this information exchange is the energy that maintains the system.
>
> 6) A system is composed of subsystems with roles which logically complement each other (p. 73-74).

Adoption of family systems theory as a useful and unifying framework for the study of the runaway phenomenon carries important conceptual implications for research as well as for assessment, treatment, and prevention. The accepted research model in Western culture, which has developed and evolved from the logical positivist-empirical tradition, is based upon observation through sensory experience in which experimentation, hypothesis testing, dependent and independent variables, control groups, and replication are essential components. According to this tradition, scientific methodology is empirical and quantitative. Measurable, objective, quantifiable results are sought from observation and experimentation. Assumptions of this Newtonian, mechanistic research model, as set forth by Becvar and Becvar,[58] are:

> 1) Valid knowledge claims can only be based on what is observed, i.e., seen, heard, smelled, tasted, or touched.
>
> 2) Control and replication are essential, particularly relative to the goal of determining cause/effect relationships.
>
> 3) Cause/effect relationships are tied to the assumption of time as absolute.
>
> 4) A reality exists independent of us as observers.
>
> 5) The experimental method seeks to eliminate subjective judgments from the practice of science.
>
> 6) Observation serves the purpose of testing theory.
>
> 7) Theory is the goal of scientific activity. The idea of science is to subject theories to disconfirming tests.
>
> 8) Reality is a constant, static, absolute phenomenon.
>
> 9) Mind transcends a reality that is independent of mind (p. 312).

As research in psychology and the social sciences evolved, objectivity and experimental methods were applied to the study of human beings as well as to the natural world. Many models for studying the family which are consistent with this traditional research approach have been developed. As might be expected, however, there are:

> real tensions between the practice of so-called normal science in the tradition of the logical positivist-empirical school and the new systemic/cybernetic paradigm. The reality is that research in the tradition of Newtonian physics can be done on family therapy.

However, all research is necessarily research on parts of the whole that is assumed by the systemic paradigm (pp. 326-327).[59]

Lather claims that we are in a "postpositivist" era in the human sciences where there is a shift away from the belief in an absolute, objective truth and toward a view of truth as increasingly complex and subject-dependent.[60] Reflecting this shift toward a systems perspective, more and more research designs are interactive, contextual, and invite joint participation in the exploration of research issues.

Reason and Rowan[61] describe "new paradigm research" as a "collaborative, experiential, participatory research" (p. xx). Reason and Rowan contrast new paradigm research with old paradigm research and "naive inquiry." Old paradigm research refers to the model which is grounded in the assumptions of the mechanistic world view and seeks objective, quantifiable data. Naive inquiry focuses on the subjective and intuitive search for knowledge. New paradigm research, a synthesis of old paradigm research and naive inquiry, is a "systematic, rigorous search for truth" which still remains alive (p. xiii). New paradigm research is "objectively subjective" (p. xiii) and moves away from a researcher-subject relationship to a subject-subject relationship. New paradigm research is reflexive and action-oriented. It does research with people, not on people.

Qualitative research methods, according to Reason and Rowan,[62] are not new paradigm research as they move only halfway towards a new paradigm. In their view, the qualitative methods such as intensive interviewing and participant observation still stay within the old paradigm and remain essentially objective in perspective. Qualitative methods are quite different from the notions of collaborative, experiential, action-oriented, participatory research which is new paradigm research.

Heron, in Reason and Rowan,[63] describes a dimension of new paradigm research as "cooperative inquiry." In cooperative inquiry subjects contribute directly to hypothesis-making, to formulating the final conclusion, and to what goes on in between. The subject is a full fledged co-researcher and the researcher is "a co-subject participating fully in the action and experience to be researched" (p. 20). Both are actively and openly involved on the inquiry side of the research and on the action side.

New paradigm research, says Reason in Reason and Rowan, [64] moves toward supporting values of inquiry as an approach to living, and of research as involving risk-taking in living. "It offers one way of ceasing to see research as the prerogative of academics, and offers it back to people as a means of enhancing their lives and developing their capacities for self-direction" (p. 331). Traditional social science research approaches interact with persons so that they make no direct contribution to formulating the propositions which claim to be about them or to be based on what they say and/or do. New paradigm research "is a radical departure from traditional methodologies and demonstrates the possibility that research might become truly experimental, a process of living inquiry" (p. 331).[65]

New paradigm research which has an "emancipatory interest" attempts to free people not only from the domination of others, but also from their domination by forces which they themselves do not understand.[66] Lather [67] explores issues in this developing area of new paradigm research and describes its goal as encouraging "self-reflection and deeper understanding on the part of the persons being researched" as well as generating "empirically grounded theoretical knowledge", all of which leads to greater self-determination (p. 266). This "research as praxis" is research which "involves the researched in a democratized process of inquiry characterized by negotiation, reciprocity, and empowerment" (p. 257). Emancipatory research calls for approaches to research whereby both the researcher and the researched become "the changer and the changed" (p. 263).

NOTES

[1] R. Becvar and D. Becvar, *Systems Theory and Family Therapy: A Primer* (Washington, D.C.: University Press of America, 1982), p. 2.

[2] D. Becvar and R. Becvar, *Family Therapy: A Systemic Integration* (Needam Heights, MA: Allyn and Bacon, Inc., 1996).

[3] See note 2 above.

[4] See note 2 above.

[5] F. Capra, *The Turning Point* (New York: Simon and Schuster, 1982), p. 265.

[6] C. Brothers, "The Gestalt Theory of Healthy Aggression in Beyond-Control Youth," *Psychotherapy* 23 (Winter 1986): 578-585.

[7] See note 5 above.

[8] See note 6 above.

[9] See note 5 above.

[10] See note 2 above.

[11] J. Briggs and F. Peat, *The Looking Glass Universe* (New York: Simon and Schuster, 1984).

[12] See note 5 above.

[13] See note 2 above.

[14] See note 2 above.

[15] See note 2 above.

[16] See note 2 above.

[17] F. Walsh, *Normal Family Processes* (New York: The Guilford Press, 1982).

[18] See note 1 above.

[19] H. Fishman, *Treating Troubled Adolescents* (New York: Basic Books, 1988).

[20] See note 17 above.

[21] G. Bateson, *Mind and Nature* (New York: Dutton, 1979).

[22] L. Bertalanffy, *General Systems Theory* (New York: George Braziller, 1968).

[23] See note 1 above.

[24] See note 21 above.

[25] See note 17 above.

[26] L. Hoffman, *Foundations of Family Therapy* (New York: Basic Books, 1981).

[27] C. Speer, "Family Systems: Morphogenesis and Morphostasis, or Is Homeostasis Enough?," *Family Process* 9 (September 1970): 259-277.

[28] See note 17 above.

[29] See note 26 above.

[30] S. Minuchin, *Families and Family Therapy* (Cambridge: Harvrd University Press, 1974); S. Minuchin, B. Montalvo, G. Guerney, B. Rossman and F. Schumer, *Families of the Slums* (New York: Basic Books, 1967).

[31] S. Minuchin (see note 30 above).

[32] S. Minuchin (see note 30 above).

[33] P. Watzlawick, J. Weakland and R. Fisch, *Change: Principles of Problem Formation and Problem Resolution* (New York: Norton, 1974); M. Selvini Palazzoli, L. Boscolo, G. Cecchin and G. Prata, *Paradoz and Counterparadox* (New York: Aronson, 1978); J. Haley, *Problem-Solving Therapy* (San Francisco: Jossey-Bass, 1976).

[34] See note 26 above.

[35] See note 26 above.

[36] T. Brennan, D. Huizinga and D. Elliott, *The Social Psychology of Runaways* (Lexington, MA: D.C. Heath and Co., 1978).

[37] S. Wolk and J. Brandon, "Runaway Adolescents' Perceptions of Parents and Self," *Adolescence* XII (Summer 1977):175-187.

[38] T. Gulotta, "Runaway: Reality or Myth," *Adolescence* 52 (Winter 1978): 543-549.

[39] G. Adams and G. Munro, "Portrait of the North American Runaway: A Critical Review," *Journal of Youth and Adolescence* 8 (1979): 359-373.

[40] R. Young, W. Godfrey, B. Matthews and G. Adams, "Runaways: A Review of Negative Consequences," *Family Relations* 32 (1983): 275-281.

[41] See note 33 above.

[42] J. Haley, *Leaving Home* (New York: McGraw-Hill, 1980).

[43] See note 26 above.

[44] See note 26 above.

[45] See note 26 above.

[46] See note 26 above.

[47] V. Satir, *Conjoint Family Therapy* (Palo Alto: Science and Behavior Books, 1964); V. Satir, *Peoplemaking* (Palo Alto: Science and Behavior Books, 1972).

[48] A. Napier and C. Whitaker, *The Family Crucible* (New York: Harper and Row, 1978).

[49] See note 48 above.

[50] See note 33 above.

[51] See note 33 above.

[52] See note 33 above.

[53] See note 26 above.

[54] See note 33 above.

[55] See note 33 above.

[56] See note 1 above.

[57] See note 1 above.

[58] See note 2 above.

[59] See note 2 above.

[60] P. Lather, "Research As Praxis," *Harvard Educational Review* 56 (1986).

[61] P. Reason and J. Rowan, eds. *Human Inquiry--A Sourcebook of New Paradigm Research* (New York:Wiley): 1981.

[62] See note 61 above.

[63] See note 61 above.

[64] See note 61 above.

[65] See note 61 above.

[66] J. Habermas, *Knowledge and Human Interests* (Boston: Beacon, 1971).

[67] See note 60 above.

IV

Case Illustrations

It is the conceptual hypothesis of the current study that family systems theory can be a useful theoretical framework for the understanding of the complex phenomenon of runaway behavior. Virtually all the literature on runaways to date recognizes in some way the importance of the family environments of young people who run away from home. Issues such as family communication, disputes, rules, violence, and alcohol and drug abuse are given great attention in the runaway literature. These and other variables are often presented as "causes" or "reasons" for running away. As a result, the runaway phenomenon is approached from an individual, linear, cause-and-effect perspective and the question "why?" is asked again and again. Madison,[1] for example, asks "Why do teenagers run?" and lists seven principal reasons, among them family disputes, trouble at school, pregnancy, and emotional problems. Brenton[2] has a chapter entitled "Cause and Consequence: Why Kids Bolt." A chapter in Burgess[3] is entitled "Causes of Running."

This linear, cause-and-effect approach which is so prevalent in the literature has provided neither a comprehensive framework nor a coherent theory for the understanding of the many and varied views on runaways. Stierlin[4] and Fishman[5] instead adopt a systems approach toward the problems of adolescents and have provided case illustrations of family therapy, including some with adolescent runaways. The focus of both Stierlin and Fishman was principally on family systems approaches to therapy. Therefore their case illustrations were designed simply to provide one example among others of ways to approach family dynamics. It is the purpose here (a) to review these two cases as systemic illustrations of runaway issues, and (b) to go beyond the discussion provided respectively by Stierlin and Fishman to demonstrate more fully the

ways systems theory can be put into practice to understand and deal
with runaway phenomena.

Stierlin[6] speaks from a systems perspective in his
description of separation in adolescence as:

> a transactional process between two parties–parents and
> children. The process can be a gradually expanding spiral
> of mutual individuation and differentiation occurring on
> various emotional, cognitive, and moral levels.
> Optimally, this spiraling leads to relative independence
> for both parties, yet is an independence based upon
> "mature interdependence" (p. 3).

Stierlin[7] develops the concept of transactional modes
which "reflect the interplay and/or relative dominance of centripetal
and centrifugal pushes between the generations" and which are
transitive and reciprocal (p. 35). These modes:

> are transitive in that they denote the active molding of
> an offspring who is still immature, dependent, and hence
> remains captive to parental influences. . . . They are
> reciprocal in the sense that there is always a two-way
> exchange. In this exchange, the children mold and
> influence their parents as much as the latter mold and
> influence them (pp. 35-36).

In his work on the separation process of parents and
adolescents, Stierlin describes as examples several categories of
runaways. "Crisis runaways," according to Stierlin,[8] are those who
remain involved with their families and finally return home. "Above
all, their running away reflects a crisis in their and their parents'
lives" (p. 19). He describes the case of Lorainne as an example (p.
19ff).

After doing well up to age 15, suddenly "everything went
wrong" and Lorainne ran away from home overnight. The police
picked her up in an abandoned house together with several other
young people who had marijuana and LSD in their pockets and
returned her to her parents. She received warnings from them as
well as from the police and her teachers and did not run away again
for some time.

Things did not go well for Lorainne, however, and she slept
around with several boys, became involved in drug use, and skipped

school. To cover for her absences from school she forged passes and lied to her parents and school officials. Finally she ran away to a hippie commune quite a distance from home. Two and a half days later her father brought her home from the commune and the family entered therapy. Although she continued to use drugs occasionally, remained sexually active, and participated in some orgies, Lorainne and her parents began to address their family, marriage, and individual issues. It became apparent that when Lorainne was 15 and experiencing the normal developmental events of adolescence, her parents at the time "could not help burdening her with problems of their own" (p. 21).

In Stierlin's description of Lorainne's family we see such systems concepts as boundary issues and triangulation of the child coming into play. He couches his understanding of this and other families' difficulties in terms of reciprocal, circular causality when he speaks of the forces which "reside partly in the adolescent, partly in the parents and families, and partly in the relationship that holds together and pushes apart the generations" (p. 21).

It is apparent from Stierlin's description that, prior to therapy, Lorainne's parents did not successfully address whatever individual and/or marital issues were present. Perhaps Lorainne's running away served to maintain homeostasis in the family system by directing her parents' focus toward her behaviors while avoiding an escalation of their own which could threaten the survival of the system. The behavior of Lorainne's parents, through their pattern of avoiding conflicts, may likewise have served to preserve the system in a homeostatic or steady state. The behaviors of all the members of the family could be "reframed" as efforts to maintain the cohesion and viability of the family system. Maintaining homeostasis in this way, by continuing patterns of attempted solutions which themselves become problematic, would seem to be preventing the family system from responding appropriately to developmental pressures. From the systems perspective, then, these dysfunctional patterns would become the focus of therapeutic change.

In the family therapy process with Lorainne's family, an answer to the question "why?" would not, from the systems perspective, have been particularly useful or even possible. The systems concept of equifinality[9] is instead useful here as it reminds us that Lorainne's family became dysfunctional while another family may have remained well functioning in the face of similar stresses. Rather than posing the question "why?", systems theory provided an awareness of what was occurring in the family as a whole and in the family subsystems as well as a focus on what needed to happen in order for the family to move toward more healthy functioning. Information describing what was happening in the family clarified the need for the parents to deal with their own issues as parents and spouses without "triangling in" Lorainne as an attempt to relieve tensions in the parental and spouse subsystems.[10] Clearer subsystem boundaries needed to be established.

As Lorainne was experiencing the normal events of adolescent development and experimenting with behaviors to differentiate herself from her family, her parents also were experiencing the pressures of their own adult developmental phases. Symptomatic behaviors in the family system appeared as the members struggled to adjust to these normal, expected life cycle transitions. Family therapy, from the systems perspective, appeared to play a positive role in this family's becoming "unstuck" and beginning to develop clearer subsystem boundaries, to establish rules which were flexible, appropriate, and open to negotiation, and to maintain a healthy balance between dependency and autonomy so that the family unit and its members could make a more successful transition to the next life phase.[11]

In Fishman's[12] treatment of troubled adolescents, including runaways, he uses the systems concept of the "homeostatic maintainer" which he describes as "the individual or social forces that are maintaining a given problem and must therefore be included in the treatment" (p. 18). The homeostatic system, according to Fishman, can be either a positive or negative force (p. 19). With a family in crisis, for example, there can be forces which function to maintain the status quo in a way which is detrimental to the system. The forces may be keeping the system from changing appropriately as the system faces developmental pressures. Homeostasis in such cases is harmful in that it prevents the system from adapting to developmental changes and evolving into a more functional and productive system.

In addition to identifying the "homeostatic maintainer" in the treatment of troubled adolescents, Fishman[13] identifies patterns which contribute to dysfunction in the system and makes use of these patterns to plan a strategy for therapeutic treatment. Conflict avoidance is one key pattern which dysfunctional families often demonstrate. This was seen in Fishman's case illustration of the runaway adolescent in which the parents allowed their teenage daughter to leave home rather than enforce their rules. In working with this family it became clear to Fishman that the parents had their own marital conflicts. He described them as "two magnetic poles, repelling each other as I challenged them to resolve their differences and take some action to retrieve their daughter from potential danger" (p. 21). These parents avoided discussing difficult issues between them to resolve conflicts and instead directed their responses to the therapist or to the daughter in order to stay on "safe ground" (p. 21).

Fishman's[14] clinical example of therapy with a family which included an adolescent runaway was that of Maria, the 15-year-old daughter of prominent parents and the middle of five children. Her sisters were nine, twelve, and seventeen, and her brother was twenty. Maria's "categorical refusal to follow her parents' rules" (p. 63) precipitated her leaving home and moving in with a boy in a poor area of the city where she had been living for several months at the time of therapy.

With Maria's family, one of Fishman's[15] major tasks was that of changing the homeostatic mechanism that was keeping the family system "stuck in its unhappiness" (p. 70). In this particular family, the parents' pattern of conflict avoidance was identified as the homeostatic maintainer, and only when husband and wife could deal with their own conflicts directly would they then be able to deal effectively with their daughter.

Fishman's[16] approach to reworking this family system was to create a "therapy of options" (p. 61). He described this family as a rigid, inflexible system in which Maria saw no other option but to run away and escape. In therapy with Maria's family Fishman sought to distinguish between the parental and the adolescent's issues and to keep the parents in their executive position in the family hierarchy while at the same time enabling them to negotiate and develop options for the child.

The first stage in therapy of families with an adolescent runaway, according to Fishman,[17] is to enable the parents to learn to negotiate between themselves in the presence of the children. Such negotiation should serve to differentiate between parental and adolescent issues and also prepare parents for beginning to negotiate with their children.

Often unrealistic fears of both parents and adolescents can play a part in keeping the system stuck in its dysfunctional patterns.[18] Parents may fear what the adolescent might do, and the adolescent may fear actions of the parents. In Maria's family, for example, the father feared that his daughter would rebel further and perhaps become a prostitute if he asserted authority over her. And the mother was afraid that her daughter would hold a grudge against her for years to come. Fishman believes that a principal task for the therapist is the acknowledgment and handling of such fears.

In Fishman's[19] case illustration of Maria's family, the father was well established and seen as a highly successful graphic designer in a very competitive advertising agency. He feared that he might be losing his ability to handle the required technical skills, however, and was seeing a psychiatrist who was treating him for depression. The mother was facing the developmental pressures of having her children grow up and need her less and less as they gained more independence and autonomy. She had earned a bachelor's degree in anthropology, but did not believe that her prospects for employment were good. These contextual pressures in the parents' individual lives in turn stressed the marital relationship itself which in turn affected their roles as parents. These patterns reflect the circular influence of individuals, relationships, and context within which the dysfunctional behaviors were taking place.[20]

Maria's parents' relationship was described by Fishman[21] as "extremely distant", and each of their relationships with their children "differed drastically" (p. 64). The mother was the more concerned parent, and the father was initially intimidated by his daughter's threats. As Maria challenged the rules of the system, the mother became braver, and the father became more intimidated by her threats. There was no precedent for negotiation in the family, and Maria moved out when her parents told her that if she didn't follow the rules, she would have to go.

In therapy sessions with this family, Fishman's[22] challenges to the parents were met by first one and then the other parent acting as the homeostatic maintainer. The father acknowledged that negotiation was necessary, but excluded the mother from the process. Early in the therapy process, Fishman's attempts to have the parents come to an agreement were countered by the father's attempts to convince Fishman to see Maria alone. Fishman attempted to have the father "function as a co-therapist to convince his wife to join with him in bringing their daughter home" (p. 65). Here the mother would not support her husband and insisted instead that Maria should be involved in the decision. Fishman claimed, "I found myself having to constantly monitor whichever parent was carrying the baton in order to address the therapy toward neutralizing the homeostatic efforts" (p. 65).

In a family system such as Maria's, in which the parents sometimes rigidly enforce rules and at other times are extremely indulgent, an adolescent can be extremely confused about what behaviors are allowed and what are not. Maria's parents resorted to a tough, rigid response, that of telling her if she did not obey the rules she would have to leave, after having given her a great deal of freedom to do whatever she wanted. This family system needed a sense of balance to restore its stability. "What Maria needed was not extremes but a gradual development of autonomy" (p. 65).[23]

Maria's parents frequently did not exercise firm executive functions, such as establishing rules, curfews, or limits on certain behaviors. Fishman[24] believed that in order to establish functional patterns of behavior in this family, the parents had to learn to negotiate between themselves and with their daughter. He worked with Maria's family to reorganize the system so that the parents could speak "with a single voice" in challenging her (p. 67). This ability would establish clear subsystem boundaries and would move the family system toward more effective patterns of communication.

Over the course of therapy Maria's parents were able to deal with their own conflicts and fears and became empowered to deal with the challenges their daughter presented. The therapy focused on the family as "a caring place where the children had limits and a voice, a place where they could negotiate" (p. 80).[25]

In families with runaways, according to Fishman,[26] the adolescent is running away from "something very poisonous in the family context. The goal of therapy, then, is to help create a different kind of context, one from which the child will not have to escape. . . . close attention was placed on what Maria had to run back to" (p. 66). The family needed to be not only "more executive" but also "more balanced, without the discordant equivocation between the parents" from which Maria felt she had to escape (p. 66).

Effective and permanent change in Maria's family and in other families with adolescent runaways, according to Fishman:[27]

> depends on the parents' capacity to be both firm and flexible. Their foremost responsibility is to keep their

children free from harm, but this can never be
accomplished if the adolescents themselves are not
given the opportunity to be free. To the extent that the
therapist can help parents retain their executive power
while allowing their children real choices, the therapy
will be successful (p. 63).

In viewing Maria's family difficulties from a systems
perspective, again we see no need to ask "why" Maria left home.
Embracing the concept of circular causality, it would be impossible
to place blame or to identify particular "reasons" for Maria's leaving
home.[28] Instead, from the framework of family systems theory,
Maria, her parents, and the family context were viewed as a
systemic whole with each part of the system both influencing and
being influenced by every other part of the system.

The solutions which Maria's parents attempted, being
extremely indulgent in some instances and quite authoritarian in
other instances, themselves became problematic. The focus was not
on "why" Maria ran away, but rather on what needed to happen in
the family in order to change the context, or the attempted
solutions, so that more functional behavior patterns could
develop.[29] Clear boundaries, between family subsystems and
between the family and other social systems, needed to be
established.[30] The system needed to become appropriately both
open and closed, open to new information from outside the system
in the form of negotiation, and closed in the form of parental
enforcement of reasonable behavioral limits.

As Maria's parents were able to bring about a change in
their own relationship, their effectiveness in dealing with their
children also became apparent. A change in a subsystem, in this
case the parents' relationship, affected other members and the
family context as a whole.[31] From the perspective of family
systems therapy, a context evolved in which Maria, her siblings, her
parents, and the family as a whole could realize more successful
transitions to the next developmental phases. Maria's family could
be viewed, as Minuchin's model would suggest, as an average
family feeling the discomforts and difficulties of accommodating to
new circumstances.

Fishman[32] describes adolescent runaways as seeing no
other option in their rigid, inflexible family systems but to run away
and escape. Through a "therapy of negotiation" alternatives can be

effectively expanded with an ultimate goal "to establish a family system in which the child does not have to run away from home but can walk away from home at the appropriate time" (p. 62). This "functional separation", according to Fishman, requires leaving without alienation. All of the individuals must "gradually let go and then reconnect" (p. 11). The therapy should end "when options are opened not only for the child but for the parents as well, options that enable them to come to terms with the developmental issues stressing the family system" (p. 62).

NOTES

[1] A. Madison, *Runaway Teens* (New York: Lodestar Books, 1979).

[2] M. Brenton, *The Runaways* (Boston: Little, Brown, and Co., 1978).

[3] A. Burgess, *Youth At Risk: Understanding Runaway and Exploited Youth* (Washington, D.C.: National Center for Missing and Exploited Children, 1986).

[4] H. Stierlin, *Separating Parents and Adolescents,* (New York: Jason Aronson, Inc., 1981).

[5] H. Fishman, *Treating Troubled Adolescents* (New York: Basic Books, 1988).

[6] See note 4 above.

[7] See note 4 above.

[8] See note 4 above.

[9] R. Becvar and D. Becvar, *Systems Theory and Family Therapy* (Washington, D.C.: University Press of America, 1982).

[10] M. Bowen, *Family Therapy in Clinical Practice* (New York: Aronson, 1978).

[11] E. Carter and M. McGoldrick, eds., *The Family Life Cycle: A Framework for Family Therapy* (New York: Gardner Press, 1980).

[12] See note 5 above.

[13] See note 5 above.

[14] See note 5 above.
[15] See note 5 above.
[16] See note 5 above.
[17] See note 5 above.
[18] See note 5 above.
[19] See note 5 above.
[20] D. Becvar and R. Becvar, *Family Therapy: A Systemic Integration* (Needam Heights, MA: Allyn and Bacon, Inc., 1996).
[21] See note 5 above.
[22] See note 5 above.
[23] See note 5 above.
[24] See note 5 above.
[25] See note 5 above.
[26] See note 5 above.
[27] See note 5 above.
[28] See note 20 above.
[29] See note 20 above. P. Watzlawick, J. Weakland, and R. Fisch, *Change: Principles of Problem Formation and Problem Resolution* (New York: Norton, 1974).
[30] S. Minuchin, *Families and Family Therapy* (Cambridge: Harvard University Press, 1974).
[31] See note 30 above.
[32] See note 5 above.

V

Summary and Discussion

SUMMARY

The purpose of the present study was to offer a comprehensive theoretical framework from which a better understanding of the runaway phenomenon could be useful to practitioners, service providers, and researchers in their further study of runaways. The current study argues that family systems theory is such a framework.

Systems theory can be a useful metatheory, or theory of theories, which recognizes the complexity of all phenomena and accepts the usefulness of all other theories, including linear, cause and effect thinking. It may be that no single theory can, or even should, be developed to explain such a multifacted phenomenon as adolescents' running away from home. An awareness and appreciation of the relationships between and among the theories we use and the phenomena we study is essential to a systems view and essential to enhancing our understanding of the adolescent runaway.

The family is, according to Bronfenbrenner,[1] the most stable and enduring foundation through the process of human development. Becvar and Becvar[2] claim that "there seems to be abundant empirical evidence to suggest that the family system exerts the greatest influence on an individual, followed by other systems such as school, church, and work, which impact on the family" (p. 55). The importance of the family and family issues in attempting to understand the runaway phenomenon was evident from the literature reviewed in this study, but no broad, unifying conceptual framework was found. The difficulties in meaningfully studying the complex runaway phenomenon without such a comprehensive perspective were cited by a number of researchers, particularly Walker[3] and Burke and Burkhead.[4] Much of the literature reviewed employed a linear perspective and attempted to

establish cause and effect explanations. The attention given to
demographic and other statistical characteristics of families,
particularly parents, and to personality characteristics of youths
themselves seemed to suggest an attempt to create scapegoats for
runaways. Much of the research attempted to break down the
phenomenon into its smallest parts in search for a cause. Definitive
results from these efforts to demonstrate cause and effect relationships
were not found.

Walker[5] encouraged researchers to "adopt a relatively
open-minded position which recognizes the importance of both
internal and external factors in explaining runaway behavior" (pp. 33-
34). Gulotta's[6] claim that a narrowly defined understanding of
runaway behavior, "one which places responsibility for the act on
the child alone", indicates the need for a much wider study of the
complex phenomenon of running away (p. 114). Spillane-Grieco[7]
claimed that runaway behavior may not lend itself to cause-and-
effect explanations "as there are multisystems involved in the lives
of the children who leave home and of the parents" (p. 159). The
current study has presented family systems theory as a unifying and
useful framework which meaningfully addresses these difficulties in
the understanding of the runaway phenomenon.

The systems perspective is a comprehensive metatheory, or
theory about theories, which recognizes the usefulness of other
theories relative to their context. The literature has clearly shown
that the adolescent runaway phenomenon is broad and complex. It is
comprised of young people who may leave home for only a few
hours, remain very close to home, and return voluntarily, as well as
those who stay away for months or years, go far from home, and
perhaps never return. There are "floaters," "splitters," and "hard road
freaks," "rootless," "anxious," and "terrified" runaways. Some are
described as "abortive," "lonely schizoid," "crisis," or "casual"
runaways. Some have been called "runaway explorers" or "runaway
manipulators." Others have been described to run under the
"binding mode" or the "expelling mode." And still others have been
called "positive runaways," "pushouts," "well adjusted," or "double
failure" runaways. The literature has demonstrated that runaways
come from virtually all racial, ethnic, and socio-economic groups,
from nuclear and single parent families, and that both boys and girls
leave home. One predominant theme in the literature has considered
running away a normal, and in some instances healthy, act. Another
perspective is that running away is a function of disturbed family

life and that many youth leave their homes to avoid physical or psychological abuse or the experience of rejection.

Each of the theories found in the literature can be viewed as useful within the metaperspective of family systems theory. Family systems theory does not stand against the linear perspective, but includes those views in integrating and embracing the essential systems concepts of contextuality and reciprocity. An adolescent's running away from home is a "problem" only as it is understood and defined in relation to context. From the systems perspective individuals are viewed relative to context rather than as types of individuals who possess particular psychological traits. An individual is not a specific sort of person; rather, "he is a certain kind of person with me the way I am with him, or in this context" (p. 53).[8] The context includes time, place, other persons, and relationships between and among all aspects of the phenomenon. These contextual variables and the behavior(s) in question are in reciprocal, mutually influencing and on-going relationships.

In this study, key concepts of family systems theory were defined and linked to the phenomenon of runaway behavior. Case material from the work of Stierlin[9] and Fishman[10] was used to illustrate specific concepts from family systems theory. Heretofore these concepts have not been elaborated upon in as much depth with regard to the runaway phenomenon.

The concepts of circular causality and reciprocity, for example, were demonstrated in Stierlin's case description of Lorainne and her family. Lorainne's normal developmental difficulties of attaining increased identity and autonomy were occurring simultaneously as her parents were experiencing their own marital and individual difficulties. Family subsystem boundaries were blurred as the parents attempted to involve, or "triangle", Lorainne into their issues. Both Lorainne's runaway behavior and her parents' attempts to avoid their own conflicts may be viewed as maintaining homeostasis and inhibiting change toward a more functional system. Lorainne's running away could be viewed as an attempt to bring the parents together to focus on her behavior and thereby avoid a change in their own relationship which could threaten the survival of the system. The parents' moves to involve Lorainne in their issues likewise could function to inhibit change in their own marital and parental relationship patterns and to keep the system from evolving more functional patterns.

Fishman's case illustration of Maria and her family also demonstrated the concepts of circular causality and homeostasis as well as the concept of a well functioning system being both open and closed. Circular causality was evident as the contextual pressures in the lives of individual family members influenced the marital/parental subsystem which influenced the adolescent subsystem which, in turn, influenced the marital/parental subsystem. Homeostasis was maintained in this family by the parents' pattern of conflict avoidance as they failed to respond to Maria's runaway behavior by enforcing their rules. Maria's behavior could also be viewed as serving to maintain homeostasis in the family. Maria's running away enabled her parents to focus attention on her while avoiding conflicts of their own. In family therapy, Maria's parents addressed her runaway behavior and their own conflicts which enabled the evolution of a family context in which the system was both open to new information from outside the system in the form of options for Maria, and closed in the sense that limits, or boundaries, of acceptable behavior were agreed upon and enforced. The family system demonstrated openness as options for Maria were negotiated between her and her parents which included increased freedom in choosing her friends and her activities. The system evolved an appropriate degree of closedness as the parents were empowered to enforce limits on time she spent away from home and on activities which could take place at home.

In therapeutic work with these two families, the contexts in which behaviors occurred were themselves the focus of change. Stierlin and Fishman assisted these families to evolve contexts in which the adolescents' runaway behavior was no longer necessary for the survival of the system.

Fishman[11] addresses the treatment of adolescent delinquency, the violent family, incest, the suicidal adolescent, and disability within the family, as well as the runaway adolescent. He gives special attention to the identification and changing of the "homeostatic maintainer" so that a more functional system may evolve. Stierlin[12] claims that the process of separation of adolescents and parents is shaped by the interplay of centripetal and centrifugal forces in the marriage relationship and in the interactions of parent and child. Stierlin's perspectives are brought to bear upon such phenomena as schizophrenia, sociopathy, and narcissism, as well as the adolescent runaway, and he proposes family therapy as a basic approach.

It was neither Stierlin's nor Fishman's main purpose to examine in depth the concepts of family systems theory to propose it as a comprehensive framework for viewing the specific phenomenon of the adolescent runaway. The current study takes an additional step of proposing family systems theory as a useful, comprehensive, and integrative theoretical framework within which to view the adolescent runaway phenomenon which partially fills a gap in current knowledge and understanding of the phenomenon. In addition, this study proposes family systems theory as a useful model which could guide future research, treatment, and prevention efforts with adolescent runaways and their families.

DISCUSSION

Limitations of the Present Study

The current study used an historical, theoretical, and case study design for the purpose of demonstrating family systems theory as a useful model in which to view the adolescent runaway phenomenon. As a result, it did not involve human subjects and was not designed to provide either quantitative or qualitative data on runaways.

The present study also focused on the traditional family constellation of mother, father, and children. The systems approach is equally applicable to the study of other family forms, such as single parent families and blended families. Case material demonstrating this applicability could further demonstrate the usefulness of family systems theory in understanding the runaway phenomenon in nontraditional family settings.

Recommendations for Future Treatment, Prevention, and Research

A major focus of this study has been family therapy as an appropriate treatment modality for families which have an adolescent runaway member. Family therapy is practiced either in community based social service agencies or in the private sector. Even though the term "family therapy" may appear to imply involvement of all members of the nuclear family, it can, in fact, be practiced with any subsystem of the family, including an individual.

One of the major assumptions of systems thinking is that a change in any part of the system constitutes a change in the system as a whole.

Logically consistent with a systems view is a recognition of the importance of the connections and interactions of adolescents and their families with other social systems such as peers, school, and community. Many of the suggestions for research, treatment, and prevention which emerged from the literature on runaways appear to be consistent with this view and should be pursued and/or continued. Walker[13] for example, concluded that adolescents' running away should be considered a family problem and resolved within the family with the help of social service agencies. Treatment for runaways and their families at community-based shelters, especially where 24-hour emergency support is available, was strongly advocated by Hughes, Comer, The National Network, Morgan, and Walker.[14] Comer[15] said that there are too few shelters and youth-protection programs and fewer independent living programs for older teens who do not have the option of returning to their families. These observations suggest a need for more community shelter service programs and adequate alternative independent living programs for runaways who find it impossible to return home.

Hersch[16] says that runaways often become involved in prostitution, are increasingly at risk for contracting AIDS, and may suffer neurophysiological impairment associated with drug use. Janus, Burgess and McCormack[17] refer to high rates of both physical and sexual abuse and suggest that a runaway event may be related to serious trauma which would require more serious clinical and social consideration. Hersch[18] notes that few of the country's shelters for runaways have on-site medical facilities, however, which suggests a need for such facilities.

Many schools and communities provide services for youth, according to Christopher, Kurtz and Howing, but troubled teenagers are often unaware of them and/ or are reluctant to use them.[19] "The logical starting point for linking youth to mental health services is the school" (p.170). Kammer and Schmidt[20] believe that school counselors can play a useful role in making proper referrals for runaways and potential runaways and their families to community service agencies and can serve as valuable links between the families and the school and community service agencies. All of these observations seem to highlight the importance of the interrelationships of treatment efforts between and among medical, social, school, and psychological services. Each of these systems can play a vital service role for runaways and their families. Effective relationships and coordination of services among these various systems would only seem to enhance the quality of service provided. Without such coordination youth will find themselves, as Ianni[21] warned, "individually and collectively *alone* amidst a maze of institutional contexts which alternatively compete for primacy in authority and protest their inability to deal with the task alone" (p. 261).

The positive roles which peer listeners and peer support groups, as well as school counselors, can play in interactions with runaways and potential runaways have been outlined by Kammer and Schmidt.[22] Goldmeier and Dean[23] suggested that peer helper programs could facilitate the development of basic trust between a trained peer listener and a potential runaway and could lessen feelings of rejection from others and from the school environment. Loeb, Burke and Boglarsky, and Wolk and Brandon[24] also believed that runaways can benefit from improved interpersonal relationship skills which can be learned in school in programs under the guidance of a school counselor. Building positive coping skills and relationship skills, promoting a sense of belonging, developing a clearer sense of self, and assisting the development of positive friendships could be outcomes of school-based programs which may be powerful deterrents to running away.[25] The positive influence which such school-based activities can have seems evident by the increasing numbers of schools which are forming peer helper programs and participating in state and national peer helper organizations.

Nye[26] suggested that another survey, similar to the 1976 Opinion Research Corporation survey, be carried out in 1981. Such a national survey was not conducted at that time, nor has one been conducted up to the present. Such a survey conducted during the 1990s could provide important quantitative trend data at the societal level and useful new information on how the runaway phenomenon has developed during the intervening years.

Recommendations for research, treatment, and prevention which appear to be consistent with a family systems perspective have emerged from the literature on runaways and deserve continued attention. Some of these recommendations may be summarized within the following areas of need:

1) more community shelter service programs and adequate independent living programs for runaways who cannot return home;

2) on-site medical facilities at shelters for runaways;

3) enhancement of the interrelationships between and among medical, social, school, and psychological services provided for runaways and their families;

4) enhancement of the positive roles which school counselors, peer listeners, and peer support groups can play in interactions with runaways and potential runaways; and

5) data on societal trends in the runaway phenomenon which have occurred since the 1976 Opinion Research Corporation survey.

In addition, studies using new paradigm and/or qualitative research designs which focus on the specific experiences of individual runaway youth and their families prior to, during, and after running away may be useful in the further study of the runaway phenomenon. These designs would focus on the runaway youth in context. Such research could provide information with regard to experiences and relationships with the family, school, peer, and other systems with which youth interface, and could be useful in the development of appropriate intervention and prevention strategies at the individual, family, school, and community levels.

A family systems research perspective suggests addressing certain key questions in the study of runaways and their families: What behavior/communication patterns are taking place in the family which may themselves be inhibiting healthy family functioning? What changes need to take place which would allow the family to evolve more functional patterns? Are the family system boundaries appropriately open and closed in relation to its sociocultural context? Are the family subsystem boundaries clear enough and flexible enough to allow for appropriate differentiation of individual family members and other subsystems as well as appropriate relationship ties between and among them? Does the family context provide an appropriate balance of both change (morphogenesis) and stability (morphostasis) which is necessary to the healthy functioning of the family system?

Further, emancipatory research which assists people in experiencing greater freedom from influences which they themselves may not understand could prove useful with adolescent runaways and their families. Both the researcher and the persons being researched could together develop emancipatory methodologies which would encourage self-reflection and deeper understanding on the part of all participants. Such research efforts could be carried out in long term placement facilities such as group homes and halfway houses as well as with runaways who return home. These efforts could, as Reason and Rowan[27] suggest, give research back to people "as a means of enhancing their lives and developing their capabilities for self-direction" (p. 331).

Becvar and Becvar[28] suggest that assessment is most useful when it describes what needs to happen in the family rather than what's wrong with the family. "Assessment which helps a family decide a direction for therapy transforms the therapy experience into a developmental process in which the family members learn to be different with one another in the different context created by the therapist" (p. 74). The following, according to Becvar and Becvar, seem to be keys to the successful functioning of family systems and help define "what would be right" processes:

1) A legitimate source of authority, established and supported over time;

2) A stable rule system established and consistently acted upon;

3) Stable and consistent shares of nurturing behavior;

4) Effective and stable child rearing and marriage and maintenance practices;

5) A set of goals toward which the family and each individual works;

6) Sufficient flexibility and adaptability to accommodate
normal developmental challenges as well as unexpected
crises (p. 74).

Family therapy, according to Becvar and Becvar[29] is a
misnomer. "Relationship therapy would be a more suitable label" (p.
326). A general goal of family therapy, or "relationship therapy," for
Becvar and Becvar[30] is to help a family evolve a context in which
symptomatic behavior on the part of an individual is not necessary
for the continued existence of the system. According to this
viewpoint, the therapist's or counselor's goals "include primary
prevention activities, or relationship development, in the form of
marriage and family development and enrichment, as well as
relationship remediation and rehabilitation, or marriage and family
therapy" (p. 56).[31]

Becvar and Becvar[32] do not challenge the usefulness of
the methodology consistent with the positivist-empirical research
tradition. They suggest that, like the systems world view, "it is but *a*
way of knowing, not *the* way of knowing. . . . We would insist that
whatever methodologies we create be logically consistent with the
assumptions of the paradigm we are using" (p. 299). In doing
research (or assessment or therapy or prevention) from the systems
perspective, according to Becvar and Becvar, family therapists and
family therapy researchers "are called upon to delineate the context
of problems as well as that of their search for solutions. . . . we must
acknowledge our lack of certainty and specify the limits of what we
can ethically claim to know" (p. 304). Therapy for Becvar and
Becvar would be "a reciprocal, qualitative process in which the
client and therapist form a partnership to explore at higher levels of
abstraction the different pragmatic explanations available . . . The
goal would be to evolve together with the client a higher order
solution to the problem as posed" (p. 303).

The recommendations for research, treatment, and
prevention which have emerged from the literature on runaways in
this study, as well as research, treatment and prevention
methodologies which have yet to be developed, should be reviewed
for consistency within the framework and guidance of family
systems theory. Logically consistent with the systems view is the
assumption that treatment, prevention, and research efforts may be
overlapping and intertwined. Interventions which are therapeutic for
one family or person or other family subsystem may be preventive

for another, or the same interventions may be both therapeutic and preventive at the same time. In addition, the same treatment and/or prevention strategies may also serve a research function.

<hr>

NOTES

[1] U. Bronfenbrenner, *The Ecology of Human Development* (Cambridge, MA: Harvard University Press, 1979).

[2] R. Becvar and D. Becvar, *Systems Theory and Family Therapy: A Primer* (Washington, D.C.: University Press of America, 1982).

[3] D. Walker, *Runaway Youth: Annotated Bibliography and Literature Overview* (Office of Social Services and Human Development, Department of Health and Human Services, 1975).

[4] W. Burke and E. Burkhead, "Runaway Children in America: A Review of the Literature," *Education and Treatment of Children* 12 (February 1989): 73-81.

[5] See note 3 above.

[6] T. Gulotta, "Leaving Home: Family Relationships of the Runaway Child," *Social Casework: The Journal of Contemporary Social Work* (February 1979): 111-114.

[7] E. Spillane-Grieco, "Feelings and Perceptions of Parents of Runaways," *Child Welfare* LXIII (March-April 1984): 159-166.

[8] See note 2 above.

[9] H. Stierlin, *Separating Parents and Adolescents* (New York: Jason Aronson, Inc., 1981).

[10] H. Fishman, *Treating Troubled Adolescents* (New York: Basic Books, 1988).

[11] See note 10 above.

[12] See note 9 above.

[13] See note 3 above.

[14] E. Hughes, "Running Away: A 50-50 Chance To Survive?:, *USA Today Magazine* 118 (September 1989):64-66; J. Comer, "Kids on the Run," *Parents* (January 1988): 146; *To Whom Do They Belong?: A Profile of America's Runaway Youth and the*

Programs That Help Them (Washington, D.C.: The National Network of Runaway and Youth Services, Inc., 1985); O. Morgan, "Runaways: Jurisdiction, Dynamics, and Treatment," *Journal of Marital and Family Therapy* (January 1982): 121-127; See note 3 above.

[15] See note 14 above.

[16] P. Hersch, "Coming of Age On City Streets,"*Psychology Today* 22 (January 1988): 28-32.

[17] M. Janus, A. Burgess and A. McCormack, "Histories of Sexual Abuse in Adolescent Male Runaways," *Adolescence* 22 (Summer 1987): 405-417.

[18] See note 16 above.

[19] G Christopher, P. Kurtz and P. Howing, "Status of Mental Health Services for Youth in School and Community," *Children and Youth Services Review* 11 (1989): 159-174.

[20] P. Kammer and D. Schmidt, "Counseling Runaway Adolescents," *The School Counselor* 35 (American School Counselor Association, Fall 1987).

[21] F. Ianni, *The Search for Structure: A Report On American Youth Today* (New York: Free Press, 1989).

[22] See note 20 above.

[23] J. Goldmeier and R. Dean, "The Runaway: Person, Problem, or Situation?", *Crime and Delinquency* (October 1973): 539-544.

[24] R. Loeb, T. Burke and C. Boglarsky, "A Large-Scale Comparison of Perspectives On Parenting Between Teenage Runaways and Nonrunaways," *Adolescence* XXI (Winter 1986): 921-930; S. Wolk and J. Brandon, "Runaway Adolescents' Perceptions of Parents and Self," *Adolescence* XII (Summer 1977): 175-187.

[25] G. Adams, T. Gulotta, and M. Clancy, "Homeless Adolescents: A Descriptive Study of Similarities and Differences Between Runaways and Throwaways," *Adolescence XX* (Fall 1985): 715-724; See note 20 above; A. Roberts, *Runaways and Nonrunaways in an American Suburb* (New York: The John Jay Press, 1981); See note 7 above; S. Wolk and J. Brandon (see note 24 above).

[26] F. Nye, "A Theoretical Perspective On Running Away," *Journal of Family Issues* 1 (June 1980): 274-299.

[27] P. Reason and J. Rowan, eds., *Human Inquiry–A Sourcebook of New Paradigm Research* (New York: Wiley, 1981).

28 See note 2 above.

29 D. Becvar and R. Becvar, *Family Therapy: A Systemic Integration* (Needam Heights, MA: Allyn and Bacon, Inc., 1996).

30 See note 2 above.

31 See note 2 above.

32 See note 29 above.

BIBLIOGRAPHY

Adams, G., T. Gulotta and M. Clancy, "Homeless Adolescents: A Descriptive Study of Similarities and Differences Between Runaways and Throwaways," *Adolescence* XX (Fall 1985): 715-724.

Adams, G. and G. Munro, "Portrait of the North American Runaway: A Critical Review," *Journal of Youth and Adolescence* 8 (1979): 359-373.

Ambrosino, L., *Runaways* (Boston: Beacon, 1971).

Bateson, G., *Mind and Nature* (New York: Dutton, 1979).

Bateson, G., *Steps to an Ecology of Mind* (New York: Ballantine, 1972).

Becvar, D. and R. Becvar, *Family Therapy: A Systemic Integration* (Needam Heights, MA: Allyn and Bacon, Inc., 1996).

Becvar, R. and D. Becvar, *Systems Theory and Family Therapy: A Primer* (Washington, D.C.: University Press of America, 1982).

Berman, C., "The Runaway Crisis," *McCall's* 115 (January 1988): 113-116.

Bertalanffy, L., *General System Theory* (New York: George Braziller, 1968).

Blood, L. and R. D'Angelo, "A Progress Research Report On Value Issues in Conflict Between Runaways and Their Parents," *Journal of Marriage and the Family* (August 1974): 486-491.

Bowen, M., *Family Therapy in Clinical Practice* (New York: Aronson, 1978).

Brennan, T., "Mapping the Diversity Among Runaways: A Descriptive Multivariate Analysis of Selected Social Psychological Background Conditions," *Journal of Family Issues* 1 (June 1980): 189-209.

Brennan, T., D. Huizinga and D. Elliott, *The Social Psychology of Runaways* (Lexington, MA: D.C. Heath and Co., 1978).

Brenton, M., *The Runaways* (Boston: Little, Brown, and Co., 1978).

Briggs, J. and F. Peat, *The Looking Glass Universe* (New York: Simon and Schuster, 1984).

Bronfenbrenner, U., *The Ecology of Human Development* (Cambridge: Harvard University Press, 1979).

Brothers, C., "The Gestalt Theory of Healthy Aggression in Beyond-Control Youth," *Psychotherapy* 23 (Winter 1986): 578-585.

Burgess, A., *Youth At Risk: Understanding Runaway and Exploited Youth* (Washington, D.C.: National Center for Missing and Exploited Children, 1986).

Burke, W. and E. Burkhead, "Runaway Children in America: A Review of the Literature," *Education and Treatment of Children* 12 (February 1989): 73-81.

Capra, F., *The Turning Point* (New York: Simon and Schuster, 1982).

Carter, E. and M. McGoldrick, eds., *The Family Life Cycle: A Framework for Family Therapy* (New York: Gardner Press, 1980).

Christopher, G., P. Kurtz and P. Howing, "Status of Mental Health Services for Youth in School and Community," *Children and Youth Services Review* 11 (1989): 159-174.

Comer, J., "Kids On the Run," *Parents* (January 1988): 146.

Crespi, D. and R. Sabatelli, "Adolescent Runaways and Family Strife: A Conflict-Induced Differentiation Framework," *Adolescence* 28 (Winter 1993): 867-878.

Dunford, F. and T. Brennan, "A Taxonomy of Runaway Youth," *Social Service Review* (September 1976): 457-470.

Edelbrock, C., "Running Away From Home: Incidence and Correlates Among Children and Youth Referred for Mental Health Services," *Journal of Family Issues* 1 (June 1980): 219-229.

Englander, S., "Some Self-Reported Correlates of Runaway Behavior in Adolescent Females," *Journal of Consulting and Clinical Psychology* 52 (1984): 484-485.

English, C., "Leaving Home: A Typology of Runaways," *Society* 10 (July/August 1973): 22-25.

Fishman, H., *Treating Troubled Adolescents* (New York: Basic Books, 1988).

Fors, S. and D. Rojek, "A Comparison of Drug Involvement Between Runaways and School Youths," *Journal of Drug Education* 21 (1991): 13-25.

Goldmeier, J. and R. Dean, "The Runaway: Person, Problem, or Situation?," *Crime and Delinquency* (October 1973): 539-544.

Gottlieb, D. and Chafetz, "Dynamics of Familial, Generational Conflict and Reconciliation," *Youth and Society* 9 (December 1977): 213-224.

Gulotta, T., "Leaving Home: Family Relationships of the Runaway Child," *Social Casework: The Journal of Contemporary Social Work* (February 1979): 111-114

Gulotta, T., "Runaway: Reality or Myth," *Adolescence* 52 (Winter 1978): 543-549.

Gutierres, S. and R. Reich, "A Developmental Perspective On Runaway Behavior: Its Relationship To Child Abuse," *Child Welfare* LX (February 1981): 89-94.

Habermas, J., *Knowledge and Human Interests* (Boston: Beacon, 1971).

Haley, J., *Leaving Home* (New York: McGraw-Hill, 1980).

Haley, J. *Problem-Solving Therapy* (San Francisco: Jossey-Bass, 1976).

Hersch, P. "Coming Of Age On City Streets," *Psychology Today* 22 (January 1988): 28-32.

Hoffman, L., *Foundations of Family Therapy* (New York: Basic Books, 1981).

Homer, L, "Community Based Resource For Runaway Girls," *Social Casework* 54 (1973): 473-479.

Howell, M., E. Emmons and D. Frank, "Reminiscences of Runaway Adolescents," *American Journal of Orthopsychiatry* 43 (October 1973): 840-853.

Hughes, E., "Running Away: A 50-50 Chance To Survive?," *USA Today Magazine* 118 (September 1989): 64-66.

Ianni, F., *The Search For Structure: A Report On American Youth Today* (New York: Free Press, 1989).

Janus, M., A. Burgess and A. McCormack, "Histories of Sexual Abuse in Adolescent Male Runaways," *Adolescence* 22 (Summer 1987): 405-417.

Jenkins, R., "Classification of Behavior Problems of Children," *American Journal of Psychiatry* 125 (February 1969): 68-75.

Jenkins, R., "The Runaway Reaction," *American Journal of Psychiatry* 128 (1971): 60-65.

Jessor, R. and S. Jessor, *Problem Behavior and Psychological Development: A Longitudinal Study of Youth* (New York: Academic Press, 1977).

Johnson, N. and R. Peck, "Sibship Composition and the Adolescent Runaway Phenomenon," *Journal of Youth and Adolescence* 7 (1978): 301-306.

Johnson, R. and M. Carter, "Flight of the Young: Why Children Run Away From Their Homes," *Adolescence* Vol. XV (Summer 1980): 483-489.

Jorgensen, S., H. Thornberg and J. Williams, "The Experience Of Running Away: Perceptions of Adolescents Seeking Help In A Shelter Care Facility," *High School Journal* (December 1980): 87-96.

Justice, B. and D. Duncan, "Running Away: An Epidemic Problem of Adolescence," *Adolescence* XI (Fall 1976): 365-371.

Kammer, P. and D. Schmidt, "Counseling Runaway Adolescents," *The School Counselor* 35 (November 1987).

Kurtz, P., G. Kurtz and J. Jarvis, "Problems of Maltreated Runaway Youth," *Adolescence* 26 (American School Counselor Association, Fall 1991): 543-555.

Lather, P., "Research As Praxis," *Harvard Educational Review* 56 (1986).

Libertoff, K., "The Runaway Child in America: A Social History," *Journal of Family Issues* 1 (June 1980): 151-164.

Loeb, R., T. Burke and C. Boglarsky, "A Large-Scale Comparison of Perspectives on Parenting Between Teenage Runaways and Nonrunaways," *Adolescence* XXI (Winter 1986): 921-930.

Madison, A., *Runaway Teens* (New York: Lodestar Books, E.D. Dutton, 1979).

Minuchin, S., *Families and Family Therapy* (Cambridge: Harvard
    University Press, 1974).

Minuchin, S., B. Montalvo, G. Guerney, B. Rosman and F.
    Schumer, *Families of the Slums* (New York: Basic Books,
    1967).

Mirkin, M., P. Raskin and F. Antognini, "Parenting, Protecting,
    Preserving: Mission of the Adolescent Female Runaway,"
    Family Process 23 (March 1984): 63-74.

Morgan, L., "Desperate Odds," *Seventeen* (March 1989): 257.

Morgan, O., "Runaways: Jurisdiction, Dynamics, and Treatment,"
    Journal of Marital and Family Therapy (January 1982): 121-
    127.

Napier, A. and C. Whitaker, *The Family Crucible* (New York:
    Harper and Row, 1978).

National Network of Runaway and Youth Services, Inc., *To Whom
    Do they Belong?: A Profile of America's Runaway Youth and
    the Programs That Help Them* (Washington, D.C.: The
    National Network of Runaway and Youth Services, Inc.,
    1985).

Nye, F., "A Theoretical Perspective On Running Away," *Journal of
    Family Issues* 1 (June 1980): 274-299.

Nye, F., *Runaways: A Report for Parents*, (Pullman, WA: Extension
    Bulletin 1743. Cooperative Extension, Washington State
    University, 1980): 1-10.

Nye, F., *Runaways: Some Critical Issues for Professionals and
    Society* (Pullman, WA: Extension Bulletin 0744.
    Cooperative Extension, Washington State University,
    1981): 1-11.

Nye, F. and C. Edelbrock, "Introduction–Some Social
    Characteristics of Runaways," *Journal of Family Issues* 1
    (June 1980): 147-150.

Olson, L., E. Liebow, F. Mannino and M. Shore, "Runaway Children Twelve Years Later: A Follow-up," *Journal of Family Issues* 1 (June 1980): 165-188.

Opinion Research Corporation, *National Statistical Survey on Runaway Youth* Report prepared for the Office of Youth Development and Office of Human Development, Department of Health, Education, and Welfare (1976).

Orten, J. and S. Soll, "Runaway Children and Their Families: A Treatment Typology," *Journal of Family Issues* 1 (June 1980): 249-261.

Ostensen, K., "The Runaway Crisis: Is Family Therapy The Answer?," *American Journal of Family Therapy* 9 (Fall 1981).

Palenski, J. and H. Launer, "The 'Process' of Running away: A Redefinition," *Adolescence* XXII (Summer 1987): 347-362.

Post, P. and D. McCoard, "Needs and Self-Concept of Runaway Adolescents," *School Counselor* 41 (January 1994): 212-219.

Rader, D. "I Want To Die So I Won't Hurt No More," *Parade* (August 2-7, 1985).

Reason, P. and J. Rowan, eds., *Human Inquiry—A Sourcebook of New Paradigm Research* (New York: Wiley, 1981).

Rich, P., "The Juvenile Justice System and Its Treatment of the Juvenile: An Overview," *Adolescence* XVII (Spring 1982): 141-152.

Roberts, A., "Adolescent Runaways In Suburbia: A New Typology," *Adolescence* XVII (Summer 1982): 387-396.

Roberts, A., *Runaways and Nonrunaways In An American Suburb* (New York: The John Jay Press, 1981).

Roberts, A., "Stress and Coping Patterns Among Adolescent Runaways," *Journal of Social Service Research* 5 (1982): 15-27.

Satir, V., *Conjoint Family Therapy* (Palo Alto: Science and Behavior Books, 1964).

Satir, V., *Peoplemaking* (Palo Alto: Science and Behavior Books, 1972).

Selvini Palazzoli, M., L. Boscolo, G. Cecchin and G. Prata, *Paradox and Counterparadox* (New York: Aronson, 1978).

Sharlin, S. and M. Mor-Barak, "Runaway Girls in Distress: Motivation, Background, and Personality," *Adolescence* 27 (Summer 1992): 387-406.

Shellow, R., J. Schamp, E. Liebow and E. Unger, "Suburban Runaways of the 1960s," *Monograph of the Society for Research in Child Development* 32 (3, Serial No. 111): 1-50.

Speck, N., D. Ginther and J. Helton, "Runaways: Who Will Run Away Again?", *Adolescence* XXIII (Winter 1988): 881-888.

Speer, C., "Family Systems: Morphogenesis and Morphostasis, or Is Homeostasis Enough?," *Family Process* 9 (September 1970): 259-277.

Spillane-Grieco, E., "Characteristics of a Helpful Relationship: A Study of Empathic Understanding and Positive Regard Between Runaways and Their Parents," *Adolescence* XIX (1984): 63-75.

Spillane-Grieco, E., "Feelings and Perceptions of Parents of Runaways," *Child Welfare* LXIII (March-April 1984): 159-166.

Stierlin, H., "A Family Perspective On Adolescent Runaways," *Archives of General Psychiatry* 29 (July 1973): 56-62.

Stierlin, H., *Separating Parents and Adolescents* (New York: Jason Aronson, Inc., 1981).

Time Magazine, "The Runaways," (September 15, 1967): 48-49.

U.S. News and World Report, "More Kids On the Road--Now It's the 'Throwaways'," (May 2, 1975).

U.S. News and World Report, "Runaways: Rising U.S. Worry," (September 3, 1973).

U.S. News and World Report, "Why Children Are Running Away In Record Numbers," (January 17, 1977): 62.

Walker, D., *Runaway Youth: Annotated Bibliography and Literature Overview* (Washington, D.C.: Office of Social Services and Human Development, Department of Health and Human Services, 1975).

Walsh, F., *Normal Family Processes* (New York: The Guilford Press, 1982).

Watzlawick, P., J. Weakland and R. Fisch, *Change: Principles of Problem Formation and Problem Resolution* (New York: Norton, 1974).

Whitaker, C. and D. Keith, "Functional Family Therapy," in A. Gurman (ed.), *Handbook of Family Therapy* (New York: Brunner-Mazel, 1988).

Wolk, S. and J. Brandon, "Runaway Adolescents' Perceptions of Parents and Self," *Adolescence* XII (Summer 1977): 175-187.

Young. R., W. Godfrey, B. Matthews and G. Adams, "Runaways: A Review of Negative Consequences," *Family Relations* 32 (1983): 275-281.

INDEX